Thomas William Robertson, Charles Farrar Browne, Edward Person Hingston

Artemus Ward's lecture

as delivered at the Egyptian Hall, London

Thomas William Robertson, Charles Farrar Browne, Edward Person Hingston

Artemus Ward's lecture
as delivered at the Egyptian Hall, London

ISBN/EAN: 9783337729035

Printed in Europe, USA, Canada, Australia, Japan

Cover: Foto ©ninafisch / pixelio.de

More available books at **www.hansebooks.com**

ARTEMUS WARD'S LECTURE.

EDITED BY HIS EXECUTORS,

T. W. ROBERTSON & E. P. HINGSTON.

WITH NUMEROUS ILLUSTRATIONS FROM THE PANORAMA.

LONDON:
JOHN CAMDEN HOTTEN, PICCADILLY.
NEW YORK:
G. W. CARLETON & CO., BROADWAY.
1869.

Entered according to Act of Congress, in the year 1869, by

G. W. CARLETON & CO.,

In the Clerk's Office of the District Court of the United States for the Southern District of New York.

CONTENTS.

	PAGE.
PORTRAIT OF CHARLES F. BROWNE.	
From bust by Gellowski	*To face title.*
FIRST ANNOUNCEMENT OF THE LECTURE	7
INTRODUCTION.	
By T. W. ROBERTSON	9
ARTEMUS WARD AS A LECTURER.	
Prefatory Note by E. P. HINGSTON	19

THE LECTURE.

By ARTEMUS WARD	57
PROSCENIUM (with the curtain down)	58
THE STEAMER "ARIEL"	74
MONTGOMERY STREET, SAN FRANCISCO	78
VIRGINIA CITY, NEVADA	82
PLAINS BETWEEN VIRGINIA AND SALT LAKE	86
PART OF SALT LAKE CITY.	
Viewed from a distance	93
SALT LAKE CITY.	
From the heights behind it	95

	PAGE.
THE SALT LAKE HOUSE	104
MAIN STREET, SALT LAKE CITY	107
THE COACH TO SALT LAKE	110
THE MORMON THEATRE	116
MAIN STREET, SALT LAKE CITY	121
UPPER PART OF MAIN STREET	125
BRIGHAM YOUNG'S PALACE	128
HEBER C. KIMBALL'S HAREM	133
TABERNACLE AND BOWERY	140
FOUNDATIONS OF THE TEMPLE	143
FOUNDATIONS OF THE TEMPLE—*continued*	145
THE TEMPLE AS IT IS TO BE	149
GREAT SALT LAKE	152
GREAT SALT LAKE—*continued*	155
CURTAIN (interval for refreshments)	158
THE ENDOWMENT HOUSE	161
ENTRANCE TO ECHO CANYON	164
THE INDIANS ON THE PLAINS	167
OUR ENCOUNTER WITH THE INDIANS	171
THE ROCKY MOUNTAINS	175
THE ROCKY MOUNTAINS SCENERY	177
THE PLAINS OF COLORADO	181
CROSSING THE PLAINS.	
An Emigrant Caravan	183

	PAGE
THE PRAIRIE ON FIRE	187
THE PRAIRIE ON FIRE—*continued*	189
BRIGHAM YOUNG AT HOME	192
THE	197

APPENDIX.

THE "*TIMES*" CRITIQUE ... Lecture

...... Artemus Ward
         At the Egyptian Hall, London ... 203

P......
         Egyptian Hall, London ... 209

THE Lecture on the Mormons was thus announced to the public of New York, when Artemus Ward first appeared at Dodworth Hall:—

THE Festivities at Dodworth Hall will be commenced by the pianist, a gentleman who used to board in the same street with Gottschalk. The man who kept the boarding-house remembers it distinctly. The overture will consist of a medley of airs, including the touching new ballads—"Dear Sister, is there any Pie in the house?" "My gentle Father, have you any Fine Cut about you?" "Mother, is the Battle o'er—and is it safe for me to come home from Canada?" And (by request of several families who haven't heard it) "Tramp, tramp, tramp, the Boys are Marching." While the enraptured ear drinks in the sweet music (we pay our pianist nine dollars a week, and "find him") the eye will be enchained by the magnificent green baize covering of the panorama. This green baize cost 40 cents a yard at Mr. Stewart's store. It was bought in deference to the present popularity of "The Wearing of the Green." We shall keep up to the times if we spend the last dollar our friends have got.

INTRODUCTION.

BY T. W. ROBERTSON.

FEW tasks are more difficult or delicate than to write on the subject of the works or character of a departed friend. The pen falters as the familiar face looks out of the paper. The mind is diverted from the thought of death as the memory recalls some happy epigram. It seems so strange that the hand that traced the jokes should be cold, that the tongue that trolled out the good things should be silent—that the jokes and the good things should remain, and the man who made them should be gone for ever.

The works of Charles Farrer Browne—who was known to the world as "Artemus Ward"—have run through so many editions, have met with such universal popularity, and have been so widely criticised, that it is needless to mention them here. So many biographies have been, written of the gentleman who wrote in the character of the 'cute Yankee Showman, that it is unnecessary that I should touch upon his life, belongings, or adventures. Of "Artemus Ward" I know just as much as the rest of the world. I prefer, therefore, to speak of Charles Farrer Browne, as I knew him, and, in doing so, I can promise those friends who also knew him and esteemed him, that as I consider no "public" man so public, that some portion of his work, pleasures, occupations, and habits may not be considered private I shall only mention how kind and noble-minded was the man of whom I write, without dragging forward special and particular acts in proof of my words, as if the goodness of his mind and character needed the certificate of facts.

I first saw Charles Browne at a literary club; he had only been a few hours in London, and he seemed highly pleased and excited at finding himself in the old city to which his thoughts had so often wandered. Browne was an intensely sympathetic man. His brain and feelings were as a "lens," and he received impressions immediately. No man could see him without liking him at once. His manner was straightforward and genial, and had in it the dignity of a gentleman, tempered, as it were, by the fun of the humorist. When you heard him talk you wanted to make much of him, not because he was "Artemus Ward," but because he was himself, for no one less resembled "Artemus Ward" than his author and creator, Charles Farrer Browne. But a few weeks ago it was remarked to me that authors were a disappointing race to know, and I agreed with the remark, and I remember a lady once said to me that the personal appearance of poets seldom "came up" to their works. To this I replied that, after all, poets were but men, and that it was as unreasonable to expect that the late Sir Walter Scott could at all resemble a Gathering of the Clans as that the late Lord Macaulay should appear anything like the Committal of the Seven Bishops to the Tower. I told the lady that she was unfair to eminent men if she hoped that celebrated engineers would look like tubular bridges, or that Sir Edwin Landseer would remind her of a "Midsummer Night's

Dream." I mention this because, of all men in the world, my friend Charles Browne was the least like a showman of any man I ever encountered. I can remember the odd half-disappointed look of some of the visitors to the Egyptian Hall when "Artemus" stepped upon the platform. At first they thought that he was a gentleman who appeared to apologise for the absence of the showman. They had pictured to themselves a coarse old man with a damp eye and a puckered mouth, one eyebrow elevated an inch above the other to express shrewdness and knowledge of the world—a man clad in velveteen and braid, with a heavy watch-chain, large rings, and horny hands, the touter to a wax-work show, with a hoarse voice, and over familiar manner. The slim gentlemen in evening dress, polished manners, and gentle voice, with the tone of good breeding that hovered between deference and jocosity ; the owner of those thin—those much too thin—white hands could not be the man who spelt joke with a " g." Folks who came to laugh, began to fear that they should remain to be instructed, until the gentlemanly disappointer began to speak, then they recovered their real "Artemus," Betsey Jane, wax-figgers, and all. Will patriotic Americans forgive me if I say that Charles Browne loved England dearly? He had been in London but a few days when he paid a visit to the Tower. He knew English history better than most Englishmen; and the Tower of London was to him the history of England embalmed in stone and mortar. No man had more reverence in his nature; and at the Tower he saw that what he had read was real. There *were* the beef-eaters; there *had* been Queen Elizabeth and Sir Walter Raleigh, and Lady Jane Grey, and Shakspere's murdered princes, and their brave, cruel uncle. There was the block and the axe, and the armour and the jewels. "St. George for merrie England!" had been shouted in the Holy Land, and men of the same blood as himself had been led against the infidel by men of the same brain and muscle as George Washington. Robin Hood was a reality, and not a schoolboy's myth like Ali Baba and Valentine and Orson.

There were two sets of feelings in Charles Browne at the

Tower. He could appreciate the sublimity of history, but, as the "Show" part of the exhibition was described to him, the humorist, the wit, and the iconoclast from the other side of the Atlantic must have smiled at the "descriptions." The "Tower" was a "show," like his own—Artemus Ward's. A price was paid for admission, and the "figgers" were "orated." Real jewellery is very like sham jewellery after all, and the "Artemus" vein in Charles Browne's mental constitution—the vein of humour, whose source was a strong contempt of all things false, mean, shabby, pretentious, and only external—of bunkum and Barnumisation—must have seen a gigantic speculation realising ship loads of dollars if the Tower could have been taken over to the States, and exhibited from town to town—the Star and Stripes flying over it—with a four-horse lecture to describe the barbarity of the ancient British Barons and the cuss of chivalry.

Artemus Ward's Lecture on the Mormons at the Egyptian Hall, Piccadilly, was a great success. His humour was so entirely fresh, new, and unconventional, it took his hearers by surprise, and charmed them. His failing health compelled him to abandon the lecture after about eight or ten weeks. Indeed, during that brief period he was once or twice compelled to dismiss his audience. I have myself seen him sink into a chair and nearly faint after the exertion of dressing. He exhibited the greatest anxiety to be at his post at the appointed time, and scrupulously exerted himself to the utmost to entertain his auditors. It was not because he was sick that the public was to be disappointed, or that their enjoyment was to be diminished. During the last few weeks of his lecture-giving, he steadily abstained from accepting any of the numerous invitations he received. Had he lived through the following London fashionable season, there is little doubt that the room at the Egyptian Hall would have been thronged nightly. Our aristocracy have a fine delicate sense of humour, and the success, artistic and pecuniary, of "Artemus Ward" would have rivalled that of the famous "Lord Dundreary." There were many stupid people who did not understand the "fun" of Artemus

Ward's books. In their vernacular "they didn't see it." There were many stupid people who did not understand the fun of Artemus Ward's lecture on the Mormons. They *could* not see it. Highly respectable people—the pride of their parish, when they heard of a lecture "upon the Mormons"—expected to see a solemn person, full of old saws and new statistics, who would denounce the sin of polygamy—and bray against polygamists with four-and-twenty boiling-water Baptist power of denunciation. These uncomfortable Christians do not like humour. They dread it as a certain personage is said to dread holy water, and for the same reason that thieves fear policemen—it finds them out. When these good idiots heard Artemus offer, if they did not like the lecture in Piccadilly, to give them free tickets for the same lecture in California, when he next visited that country, they turned to each other indignantly, and said "What use are tickets for California to *us?* We are not going to California. No! we are too good—too respectable to go so far from home. The man is a fool!" One of these ornaments of the vestry complained to the doorkeepers, and denounced the lecture as an imposition— "and," said the wealthy parishioner, "as for the panorama, it's the worst painted thing I ever saw in all my life!"

But the Entertainment, original, humorous, and racy though it was, was drawing to a close! In the fight between youth and death, death was to conquer. By medical advice Charles Browne went for a short time to Jersey— but the breezes of Jersey were powerless. He wrote to London to his nearest and dearest friends—the members of a literary club of which he was a member—to complain that his "loneliness weighed on him." He was brought back, but could not sustain the journey farther than Southampton. There the members of the beforementioned club travelled from London to see him—two at a time—that he might be less lonely—and for the unwearying solicitude of his friend and agent, Mr. Hingston, and to the kindly sympathy of the United States Consul at Southampton, Charles Browne's best and nearest friends had cause to be grateful. I cannot close these lines without mention of "Artemus

Ward's" last joke. He had read in the newspapers that a wealthy American had offered to present the Prince of Wales with a splendid yacht, American built.

"It seems," said the invalid "a fashion now-a-days for everybody to present the Prince of Wales with something. I think I shall leave him—*my Panorama!*"

Charles Browne died beloved and regretted by all who knew him, and by many who had known him but a few weeks; and when he drew his last breath there passed away the spirit of a true gentleman.

T. W. ROBERTSON.

LONDON,
August 11, 1868.

ARTEMUS WARD AS A LECTURER.

PREFATORY NOTE

BY EDWARD P. HINGSTON.

IN Cleveland, Ohio, the pleasant city beside the lakes, Artemus Ward first determined to become a public lecturer. He and I rambled through Cleveland together after his return from California. He called on some old friends at the *Herald* office, then went over to the Weddel House, and afterwards strolled across to the offices of the *Plaindealer*, where, in his position as sub-editor he had written many of his earlier essays. Artemus inquired for Mr. Gray, the editor, who chanced to be absent. Looking round at the vacant desks and ink-stained furniture, Artemus was silent for a minute or two, and then burst into one of those peculiar chuckling fits of laughter in which he would occasionally indulge; not a loud laugh, but a shaking of the whole body with an impulse of merriment which set every muscle in motion. "Here"—said he—"here's where they called me a fool." The remembrance of their so calling him seemed to afford him intense amusement.

From the office of the *Cleveland Plaindealer* we continued our tour of the town. Presently we found ourselves in front of Perry's statue, the monument erected to commemorate the naval engagement on Lake Erie, wherein the Americans came off victorious. Artemus looked up to the statue, laid his finger to the side of his nose, and in his quaint manner remarked, "I wonder whether they called him 'a fool' too, when he went to fight?"

The remark, following close as it did upon his laughing fit in the newspaper office, caused me to inquire why he had been called "a fool," and who had called him so.

"It was the opinion of my friends on the paper," he replied; "I told them that I was going in for lecturing.

They laughed at me and called me 'a fool.' Don't you think they were right?"

Then we sauntered up Euclid Street, under the shade of its avenue of trees. As we went along, Artemus Ward recounted to me the story of his becoming a lecturer. Our conversation on that agreeable evening is fresh in my remembrance. Memory still listens to the voice of my companion in the stroll, still sees the green trees of Euclid Street casting their shadows across our path, and still joins in the laugh with Artemus, who, having just returned from California, where he had taken 1600 dollars at one lecture, did not think that to be evidence of his having lost his senses.

The substance of that which Artemus Ward then told me, was that while writing for the *Cleveland Plaindealer* he was accustomed, in the discharge of his duties as a reporter, to attend the performances of the various minstrel troupes and circuses which visited the neighbourhood. At one of these he would hear some story of his own, written a month or two previously, given by the "middle-man" of the minstrels and received with hilarity by the audience. At another place he would be entertained by listening to jokes of his own invention, coarsely retailed by the clown of the ring and shouted at by the public as capital waggery on the part of the performer. His own good things from the lips of another "came back to him with alienated majesty" as Emerson expresses it. Then the thought would steal over him—why should that man gain a living with my witticisms, and I not use them in the same way myself? why not be the utterer of my own coinage, the quoter of my own jests, the mouth-piece of my own merry conceits? Certainly it was not a very exalted ambition, to aim at the glories of a circus-clown or the triumphs of a minstrel with a blackened face. But, in the United States a somewhat different view is taken of that which is fitting and seemly for a man to do, compared with the estimate we form in this country. In a land where the theory of caste is not admitted, the relative respectability of the various profession is not quite the same as it with us. There the profession does not disqualify if the man himself be right, nor the claim to the title of gentleman depend upon the avocation followed. I know of one or two clowns in the ring who are educated physicians, and not thought to be any the less gentleman because they propound conundrums and perpetrate jests instead of prescribing pills and potions.

Artemus Ward was always very self-reliant; when once he believed himself to be in the right it was almost impossible to persuade him to the contrary. But, at the same time he was cautious in the extreme, and would well consider his position before deciding that which was right or wrong for him to do. The idea of becoming a public man having taken possession of his mind, the next point to decide was in what form he should appear before the public. That of a humorous lecturer seemed to him to be the best. It was unoccupied ground. America had produced entertainers who by means of facial changes or eccentricities of costume had contrived to amuse their audiences, but there was no one who ventured to joke for an hour before a house full of people with no aid from scenery or dress. The experiment was one which Artemus resolved to try. Accordingly, he set himself to work to collect all his best quips and cranks, to invent what new drolleries he could, and to remember all the good things that he had heard or met with. These he noted down and strung together almost without relevancy or connection. The manuscript chanced to fall into the hands of the people at the office of the newspaper on which he was then employed, and the question was put to him of what use he was going to make of the strange jumble of jest which he had thus compiled. His answer was that he was about to turn lecturer, and that before them were the materials of his lecture. It was then that his friends laughed at him, and characterised him as "a fool."

"They had some right to think so," said Artemus to me as we rambled up Euclid Street. "I half thought that I was one myself. I don't look like a lecturer—do I?"

He was always fond, poor fellow, of joking on the subject of his personal appearance. His spare figure and tall stature, his prominent nose and his light-coloured hair were each made the subject of a joke at one time or another in the course of his lecturing career. If he laughed largely at the foibles of others, he was equally disposed to laugh at any shortcomings he could detect in himself. If anything at all in his outward form was to him a source of vanity, it was the delicate formation of his hands. White, soft, long, slender, and really handsome, they were more like the hands of a high-born lady than those of a western editor. He attended to them with careful pride, and never alluded to them as a subject for his jokes, until, in his last illness they had become unnaturally fair, translucent, and attenuated. Then it was that a friend calling upon him at his apartments in Piccadilly, endeavoured to cheer him at a time of great mental depression, and pleasantly reminded him of a ride they had long ago projected through the south-western states of the Union. "We must do that ride yet, Artemus. Short stages at first, and longer ones as we go on." Poor Artemus lifted up his pale, slender hands, and letting the light shine through them, said jocosely, "Do you think these would do to hold a rein with? Why, the horse would laugh at them."

Having collected a sufficient number of quaint thoughts, whimsical fancies, bizarre notions, and ludicrous anecdotes, the difficulty which then, according to his own confession, occurred to Artemus Ward was, what should be the title of his lecture. The subject was no difficulty at all, for the simple reason that there was not to be any. The idea of instructing or informing his audience never once entered into his plans. His intention was merely to amuse; if possible keep the house in continuous laughter for an hour and-a-half, or rather an hour and twenty minutes, for that was the precise time, in his belief, which people could sit to listen and to laugh without becoming bored; and, if possible, send his audience home well pleased with the lecturer and with themselves, without their having any clear idea of that which they had been listening to, and not one jot the wiser than when they came. No one better understood than Artemus the wants of a miscellaneous audience who paid their dollar or half-dollar each to be amused. No one could gauge better than he the capacity of the crowd to feed on pure fun, and no one could discriminate more clearly than he the fitness, temper, and mental appetite of the constituents of his evening assemblies. The prosiness of an ordinary Mechanics' Institute lecture was to him simply abhorrent, the learned platitudes of a professed lecturer were to him, to use one of his own phrases, "worse than poison." To make people laugh was to be his primary endeavour. If in so making them laugh he could also cause them to see through a sham, be ashamed of some silly national prejudice or suspicions of the value of some current piece of political bunkum, so much the better. He believed in laughter as thoroughly wholesome, he had the firmest conviction that fun is healthy, and sportiveness the truest sign of sanity. Like Talleyrand, he was of opinion that, "*Qui rit sans folie n'est pas si sage qu'il croit.*"

Artemus Ward's first lecture was entitled "The Babes in the Wood." I asked him why he chose that title, because there was nothing whatever in the lecture relevant to the subject of the child-book legend. He replied, "It seemed to sound the best. I once thought of calling the lecture 'My Seven Grandmothers.' Don't you think that would have been good?" It would at any rate have been just as pertinent. Incongruity as an element of fun was always an idea uppermost in the mind of the western humorist. I am not aware that the notes of any of his lectures, except those of his Mormon experience, have been preserved, and I have some doubts if any one of his lectures, except the Mormon one, was ever fairly written out. "The Babes in the Wood" as a lecture was a pure and unmitigated "sell." It was merely joke after joke, and drollery succeeding to drollery, without any connecting thread whatever. It was an exhibition of fireworks, owing half its brilliancy and more than half its effect to the skill of the man who grouped the fireworks together and let them off. In the hands of any other pyrotechnist the squibs would have failed to light, the rockets would have refused to ascend, and the "nine-bangers" would have exploded but once or twice only, instead of nine times. The artist of the display being no more, and the fireworks themselves having gone out, it is perhaps not to be regretted that the cases of the squibs and the tubes of the rockets have not been carefully kept. Most of the good things introduced by Artemus Ward in his first lecture were afterwards incorporated by him in subsequent writings, or used over again in his later entertainment. Many of them had reference to the events of the day, the circumstances of the American War and the politics of the Great Rebellion. These of course have lost their interest with the passing away of the times which gave them birth. The points of many of the jokes have corroded, and the barbed head of many an arrow of Artemus's wit has rusted into bluntness with the decay of the bow from which it was propelled.

If I remember rightly, the "Babes in the Wood" were never mentioned more than twice in the whole lecture. First, when the lecturer told his audience that the "Babes" were to constitute the subject of his discourse, and then digressed immediately to matters quite foreign to the story. Then again at the conclusion of the hour and twenty minutes of drollery, when he finished up in this way: "I now come to my subject—'The Babes in the Wood.'" Here he would take out his watch, look at it with affected surprise, put on an appearance of being greatly perplexed, and amidst roars of laughter from the people, very gravely continue, "But I find that I have exceeded my time, and will therefore merely remark that so far as I know they were very good babes—they were as good as ordinary babes. I really have not time to go into their history. You will find it all in the story-books. They died in the woods, listening to the woodpecker tapping the hollow beech-tree. It was a sad fate for them, and I pity them. So, I hope, do you. Good night!"

Artemus gave his first lecture at Norwich in Connecticut, and travelled over a considerable portion of the Eastern States before he ventured to give a sample of his droll oratory in the Western Cities, wherein he had earned reputation as a journalist. Gradually his popularity became very great, and in place of letting himself out at so much per night to literary societies and athenaeums, he constituted himself his own showman, engaging that indispensable adjunct to all showmen in the United States, an agent to go ahead, engage halls, arrange for the sale of tickets, and engineer the success of the show. Newspapers had carried his name to every village of the Union, and his writings had been largely quoted in every journal. It required, therefore, comparatively little advertising to announce his visit to any place in which he had to lecture. But it was necessary that he should have a bill or poster of some kind. The one he adopted was simple, quaint, striking, and well adapted to the purpose. It was merely one large sheet, with a black ground, and the letters cut out in the block, so as to print white. The reading was "ARTEMUS WARD WILL SPEAK A PIECE." To the American mind this was intensely funny from its childish absurdity. It is customary in the States for children to speak or recite "a piece" at school at the annual examination, and the phrase is used just in the same sense as in England we say "a Christmas piece." The professed subject of the lecture being that of a story familiar to children, harmonized well with the droll placard which announced its delivery. The place and time were notified on a slip pasted beneath. To emerge from the dull depths of lyceum committees and launch out as a showman-lecturer on his own responsibility was something both novel and bold for Artemus to do. In the majority of instances he or his agent met with speculators who were ready to engage him for so many lectures, and secure to the lecturer a certain fixed sum. But in his later transactions Artemus would have nothing to do with them, much preferring to undertake all the risk himself. The last speculator to whom he sold himself for a tour was, I believe, Mr. Wilder, of New York City, who realized a large profit by investing in lecturing stock, and who was always ready to engage a circus, a wild-beast show, or a lecturing celebrity.

As a rule, Artemus Ward succeeded in pleasing every one in his audience, especially those who understood the character of the man and the drift of his lecture; but there were not wanting at any of his lectures a few obtuse-minded, slowly-perceptive, drowsy-headed dullards, who had not the remotest idea what the entertainer was talking about, nor why those around him indulged in laughter. Artemus was quick to detect these little spots upon the sunny face of his auditory. He would pick them out, address himself at times to them especially, and enjoy the bewilderment of his Bœotian patrons. Sometimes a stolid inhabitant of central New York, evidently of Dutch extraction, would regard him with an open stare expressive of a desire to enjoy that which was said if the point of the joke could by any possibility be indicated to him. At other times a demure Pennsylvania Quaker would benignly survey the poor lecturer with a look of benevolent pity, and, on one occasion, when my friend was lecturing at Peoria, an elderly lady, accompanied by her two daughters, left the room in the midst of the lecture, exclaiming, as she passed me at the door, "It is too bad of people to laugh at a poor young man who doesn't know what he is saying and ought to be sent to a lunatic asylum!"

The newspaper reporters were invariably puzzled in attempting to give any correct idea of a lecture by Artemus Ward. No report could fairly convey an idea of the entertainment, and being fully aware of this, Artemus would instruct his agent to beg of the papers not to attempt giving any abstract of that which he said. The following is the way in which the reporter of the *Golden Era*, at San Francisco, California, endeavoured to inform the San Franciscan public of the character of "The Babes in the Wood" lecture. It is, as the reader will perceive, a burlesque on the way in which Artemus himself dealt with the topic he had chosen; while it also notes one or two of the salient features of my friend's style of lecturing :—

"HOW ARTEMUS WARD 'SPOKE A PIECE.'"

"Artemus has arrived. Artemus has spoken. Artemus has triumphed. Great is Artemus!

"Great also is Platt's Hall. But Artemus is greater; for the hall proved too small for his audience, and too circumscribed for the immensity of his jokes. A man who has drank twenty bottles of wine may be called 'full.' A pint bottle with a quart of water in it would also be accounted full; and so would an hotel be, every bed in it let three times over on the same night to three different occupants, but none of these would be so full as Platt's Hall was on Friday night to hear Artemus Ward 'speak a piece.'

"The piece selected was 'The Babes in the Wood,' which reminds us that Mr. Ward is a tall, slender-built, fair-complexioned, jovial-looking gentleman of about twenty-seven years of age. He has a pleasant manner, an agreeable style, and a clear, distinct, and powerful voice.

"'The Babes in the Wood' is a 'comic oration,' with a most comprehensive grasp of subject. As spoken by its witty author, it elicited gusts of laughter and whirlwinds of applause. Mr. Ward is no prosy lyceum lecturer. His style is neither scientific, didactic, or philosophical. It is simply that of a man who is brimful of mirth, wit and satire, and who is compelled to let it flow forth. Maintaining a very grave countenance himself, he plays upon the muscles of other people's faces as though they were pianostrings and he the prince of pianists.

"The story of 'The Babes in the Wood' is interesting in the extreme. We would say, *en passant*, however, that Artemus Ward is a perfect steam factory of puns and a museum of American humour. Humanity seems to him to be a vast mine, out of which he digs tons of fun; and life a huge forest, in which he can cut down 'cords' of comicality. Language with him is like the brass balls with which the juggler amuses us at the circus—ever being tossed up, ever glittering, ever thrown about at pleasure. We intended to report his lecture at full, but we laughed till we split our lead pencil and our short-hand symbols were too infused with merriment to remain steady on the paper. However, let us proceed to give an idea of 'The Babes in the Wood.' In the first place it is a comic oration; that is, it is spoken, is exuberant in fun, felicitous in fancy, teeming with jokes, and sparkling as bright waters on a sunny day. The 'Babes in the Wood' is—that is, it isn't a lecture or an oratorical effort; it is something *sui generis;* something reserved for our day and generation, which it would never have done for our forefathers to have known, or they would have been too mirthful to have attended to the business of preparing the world for our coming; and something which will provoke so much laughter in our time, that the echo of the laughs will reverberate along the halls of futurity and seriously affect the nerves of future generations.

"The 'Babes in the Wood' to describe it, is—Well, those who listened to it know best. At any rate they will acknowledge with us that it was a great success; and that Artemus Ward has a fortune before him in California.

"And now to tell the story of 'The Babes in the Wood'—But we will not, for the hall was not half large enough to accommodate those who came; consequently Mr. Ward will tell it over again at the Metropolitan Theatre next Tuesday evening. The subject will again be 'The Babes in the Wood.'"

Having travelled over the Union with "The Babes in the Wood" lecture, and left his audiences everywhere fully "in the wood" as regarded the subject announced in the title, Artemus Ward became desirous of going over the same ground again. There were not wanting dreary and timid prophets who told him that having "sold" his audiences once, he would not succeed in gaining large houses a second time. But the faith of Artemus in the unsuspecting nature of the public was very large, so with fearless intrepidity he conceived the happy thought of inventing a new title, but keeping to the same old lecture, interspersing it here and there with a few fresh jokes, incidental to new topics of the times. Just at this period General McClellan was advancing on Richmond, and the celebrated fight at Bull's Run had become matter of history. The forcible abolition of slavery had obtained a place among the debates of the day, Hinton Rowan Helper's book on "The Inevitable Crisis" had been sold at every bookstall, and the future of the negro had risen into the position of being the great point of discussion throughout the land. Artemus required a very slender thread to string his jokes upon, and what better one could be found than that which he chose? He advertised the title of his next lecture as "Sixty Minutes in Africa." I need scarcely say that he had never been in Africa, and in all probability had never read a book on African travel. He knew nothing about it, and that was the very reason he should choose Africa for his subject. I believe that he carried out the joke so far as to have a map made of the African continent, and that on a few occasions, but not on all, he had it suspended in the lecture-room. It was in Philadelphia and at the Musical Fund Hall in Locust Street that I first heard him deliver what he jocularly phrased to me as "My African Revelation." The hall was very thronged, the audience must have exceeded two thousand in number, and the evening was unusually warm. Artemus came on the rostrum with a roll of paper in his hands, and used it to play with throughout the lecture, just as recently at the Egyptian Hall, while lecturing on the Mormons, he invariably made use of a lady's riding-whip for the same purpose. He commenced his lecture thus, speaking very gravely and with long pauses between his sentences, allowing his audience to laugh if they pleased, but seeming to utterly disregard their laughter.

"I have invited you to listen to a discourse upon Africa. Africa is my subject. It is a very large subject. It has the Atlantic Ocean on its left side, the Indian Ocean on its right, and more water than you could measure out at its smaller end. Africa produces blacks—ivory blacks—they get ivory. It also produces deserts, and that is the reason it is so much deserted by travellers. Africa is famed for its roses. It has the red rose, the white rose, and the neg-rose. Apropos of negroes, let me tell you a little story."

Then he at once diverged from the subject of Africa to retail to his audience his amusing story of the Conversion of a Negro, which he subsequently worked up into an article in the *Savage Club Papers*, and entitled "*Concerning the Nigger*." Never once again in the course of the lecture did he refer to Africa, until the time having arrived for him to conclude, and the people being fairly worn out with laughter, he finished up by saying, "Africa, ladies and gentlemen, is my subject. You wish me to tell you something about Africa. Africa is on the map—it is on all the maps of Africa that I have ever seen. You may buy a good map for a dollar, and if you study it well, you will know more about Africa than I do. It is a comprehensive subject, too vast, I assure you, for me to enter upon to-night. You would not wish me to, I feel that—I feel it deeply, and I am very sensitive. If you go home and go to bed it will be better for you than to go with me to Africa."

The joke about the "neg-rose" has since run the gauntlet of nearly all the minstrel bands throughout England and America. All the "bones," every "middle-man," and all "end-men" of the burnt-cork profession have used Artemus Ward as a mine wherein to dig for the ore which provokes laughter. He has been the "cause of wit in others," and the bread-winner for many dozens of black-face songsters—"singists" as he used to term them. He was just as fond of visiting their entertainments as they were of appropriating his jokes; and among his best friends in New York were the brothers Messrs. Neil and Dan Bryant, who have made a fortune by what has been facetiously termed—"the burnt-cork-opera."

It was in his "Sixty Minutes in Africa" lecture that Artemus Ward first introduced his celebrated satire on the negro, which he subsequently put into print. "The African," said he, "may be our brother. Several highly respectable gentlemen and some talented females tell me that he is, and for argument's sake I might be induced to grant it, though I don't believe it myself. But the African isn't our sister, and wife, and uncle. He isn't several of our brothers and first wife's relations. He isn't our grandfather and great grandfather, and our aunt in the country. Scarcely."

It may easily be imagined how popular this joke became when it is remembered that it was first perpetrated at a time when the negro question was so much debated as to have become an absolute nuisance. Nothing else was talked of; nobody would talk of anything but the negro. The saying arose that all Americans had "nigger-on-the-brain." The topic had become nauseous, especially to the Democratic party; and Artemus always had more friends among them than among the Republicans. If he had any politics at all he was certainly a Democrat.

War had arisen, the South was closed, and the lecturing arena considerably lessened. Artemus Ward determined to go to California. Before starting for that side of the American continent, he wished to appear in the city of New York. He engaged, through his friend Mr. De Walden, the large hall then known as Niblo's, in front of the Niblo's Garden Theatre, and now used, I believe, as the dining-room of the Metropolitan Hotel. At that period Pepper's Ghost chanced to be the great novelty of New York City, and Artemus Ward was casting about for a novel title to his old lecture. Whether he or Mr. De Walden selected that of "Artemus Ward's Struggle with a Ghost" I do not know; but I think that it was Mr. De Walden's choice. The title was seasonable and the lecture successful. Then came the tour to California, whither I proceeded in advance to warn the miners on the Yuba, the travellers on the Rio Sacramento, and the citizens of the Chrysopolis of the Pacific that "A. Ward" would be there shortly. In California the lecture was advertised under its old name of "The Babes in the Wood." Platt's Hall was selected for the scene of operation, and, so popular was the lecturer, that on the first night we took at the doors more than sixteen hundred dollars in gold. The crowd proved too great to take money in the ordinary manner, and hats were used for people to throw their dollars in. One hat broke through at the crown. I doubt if we ever knew to a dollar how many dollars it once contained.

California was duly travelled over, and "The Babes in the Wood" listened to with laughter in its flourishing cities, its mining-camps among the mountains, and its "new placers" beside gold-bedded rivers. While journeying through that strangely-beautiful land, the serious question arose—What was to be done next? After California—where?

Before leaving New York, it had been a favourite scheme of Artemus Ward not to return from California to the East by way of Panama, but to come home across the Plains, and to visit Salt Lake City by the way. The difficulty that now presented itself was, that winter was close upon us, and that it was no pleasant thing to cross the Sierra Nevada and scale the Rocky Mountains with the thermometer far below freezing point. Nor was poor Artemus even at that time a strong man. My advice was to return to Panama, visit the West India Islands, and come back to California in the spring, lecture again in San Francisco, and then go on to the land of the Mormons. Artemus doubted the feasibility of this plan, and the decision was ultimately arrived at to try the journey to Salt Lake. Unfortunately the winter turned out to be one of the severest. When we arrived at Salt Lake City, my poor friend was seized with typhoid fever, resulting from the fatigue we had undergone, the intense cold to which we had been subjected, and the excitement of being on a journey of 3,500 miles across the North American Continent, when the Pacific Railway had made little progress and the Indians were reported not to be very friendly.

The story of the trip is told in Artemus Ward's lecture. I have added to it, at the special request of the publisher, a few explanatory notes, the purport of which is to render the reader acquainted with the characteristics of the lecturer's delivery. For the benefit of those who never had an opportunity of seeing Artemus Ward nor of hearing him lecture, I may be pardoned for attempting to describe the man, himself.

In stature he was tall, in figure, slender. At any time during our acquaintance his height must have been disproportionate to his weight. Like his brother Cyrus, who died a few years before him, Charles F. Browne, our

"Artemus Ward," had the premonitory signs of a short life strongly evident in his early manhood. There were the lank form, the long pale fingers, the very white pearly teeth, the thin, fine, soft hair, the undue brightness of the eyes, the excitable and even irritable disposition, the capricious appetite, and the alternately jubilant and despondent tone of mind which too frequently indicate that "the abhorred fury with the shears" is waiting too near at hand to "slit the thin-spun life." His hair was very light-coloured, and not naturally curly. He used to joke in his lecture about what it cost him to keep it curled; he wore a very large moustache without any beard or whiskers; his nose was exceedingly prominent, having an outline not unlike that of the late Sir Charles Napier. His forehead was large, with, to use the language of the phrenologists, the organs of the perceptive faculties far more developed than those of the imaginative powers. He had the manner and bearing of a naturally-born gentleman. Great was the disappointment of many who, having read his humorous papers descriptive of his exhibition of snakes and wax-work, and who having also formed their ideas of him from the absurd pictures which had been attached to some editions of his works, found on meeting with him that there was no trace of the showman in his deportment, and little to call up to their mind the smart Yankee who had married "Betsy Jane." There was nothing to indicate that he had not lived a long time in Europe and acquired the polish which men gain by coming in contact with the society of European capitals. In his conversation there was no marked peculiarity of accent to identify him as an American, nor any of the braggadocio which some of his countrymen unadvisedly assume. His voice was soft, gentle, and clear. He could make himself audible in the largest lecture-rooms without effort. His style of lecturing was peculiar; so thoroughly *sui generis*, that I know of no one with whom to compare him, nor can any description very well convey an idea of that which it was like. However much he caused his audience to laugh, no smile appeared upon his own face. It was grave even to solemnity, while he was giving utterance to the most delicious absurdities. His assumption of indifference to that which he was saying, his happy manner of letting his best jokes fall from his lips as if unconscious of their being jokes at all, his thorough self-possession on the platform, and keen appreciation of that which suited his audience, and that which did not, rendered him well qualified for the task which he had undertaken—that of amusing the public with a humorous lecture. He understood and comprehended to a hair's breadth the grand secret of how not to bore. He had weighed, measured, and calculated to a nicety the number of laughs an audience could indulge in on one evening, without feeling that they were laughing just a little too much. Above all, he was no common man, and did not cause his audience to feel that they were laughing at that which they should feel ashamed of being amused with. He was intellectually up to the level of nine-tenths of those who listened to him, and in listening, they felt that it was no fool who wore the cap and bells so excellently. It was amusing to notice how with different people his jokes produced a different effect. The Honourable Robert Lowe attended one evening at the Mormon Lecture, and laughed as hilariously as any one in the room. The next evening Mr. John Bright happened to be present. With the exception of one or two occasional smiles, he listened with grave attention.

In placing the lecture before the public in print it is impossible by having recourse to any system of punctuation to indicate the pauses, jerky emphases, and odd inflexions of voice which characterized the delivery. The reporter of the *Standard* newspaper describing his first lecture in London aptly said, "Artemus dropped his jokes faster than the meteors of last night succeeded each other in the sky. And there was this resemblance between the flashes of his humour and the flights of the meteors, that in each case one looked for jokes or meteors, but they always came just in the place that one least expected to find them. Half the enjoyment of the evening lay, to some of those present, in, listening to the hearty cachinnation of the people who only found out the jokes some two or three minutes after they were made, and who then laughed apparently at some grave statements of fact. Reduced to paper the showman's jokes are certainly not brilliant ; almost their whole effect lies in their seemingly impromptu character They are carefully led up to, of course, but they are uttered as if they are mere afterthoughts of which the speaker is hardly sure." Herein the writer in the *Standard* hits the most marked peculiarity of Artemus Ward's style of lecturing. His affectation of not knowing what he was uttering ; his seeming fits of abstraction, and his grave melancholy aspect constituted the very cream of the entertainment. Occasionally he would amuse himself in an apparently meditative mood, by twirling his little riding-whip, or by gazing earnestly but with affected admiration at his panorama. At the Egyptian Hall his health entirely failed him, and he would occasionally have to use a seat during the course of the lecture. In the notes which follow I have tried, I know how inefficiently, to convey here and there an idea of how Artemus rendered his lecture amusing by gesture or action. I have also, at the request of the Publisher, made a few explanatory comments on the subject of our Mormon trip. In so doing I hope that I have not thrust myself too prominently forward nor been too officious in my explanations. My aim has been to add to the interest of the lecture with those who never heard it delivered, and to revive in the memory of those who did some of its notable peculiarities. The illustrations are from photographs of the panorama painted in America for Artemus, as the pictorial portion of his entertainment.

In the lecture is the fun of the journey. For the hard facts the reader in quest of information is referred to a book published previously to the lecturer's appearance at the Egyptian Hall, the title of which is, "Artemus Ward: His Travels Among the Mormons." Much against the grain as it was for Artemus to be statistical, he has therein detailed some of the experiences of his Mormon trip, with due regard to the exactitude and accuracy of statement expected by information-seeking readers in a book of travels. He was not precisely the sort of traveller to write a paper for the evening meetings of the Royal

Geographical Society, nor was he sufficiently interested in philosophical theories to speculate on the developments of Mormonism as illustrative of the history of religious belief. We were looking out of the window of the Salt Lake House one morning, when Brigham Young happened to pass down the opposite side of Main Street. It was cold weather, and the prophet was clothed in a thick cloak of some green-coloured material. I remarked to Artemus that Brigham had, seemingly, compounded Mormonism from portions of a dozen different creeds, and that in selecting green for the colour of his apparel he was imitating Mahomet. "Has it not struck you," I observed, "that Swedenborgianism and Mahometanism are oddly blended in the Mormon faith?"

"Petticoatism and plunder," was Artemus's reply; and that comprehended his whole philosophy of Mormonism. As he remarked elsewhere: "Brigham Young is a man of great natural ability. If you ask me, How pious is he? I treat it as a conundrum, and give it up."

To lecture in London, and at the Egyptian Hall, had long been a favourite idea of Artemus Ward. Some humorist has said that "All good Americans when they die——go to Paris." So do most, whether good or bad, while they are living.

Still more strongly developed is the trans-atlantic desire to go to Rome. In the far west of the Missouri, in the remoter west of Colorado, and away in far north-western Oregon, I have heard many a tradesman express his intention to make dollars enough to enable him to visit Rome. In a land where all is so new, where they have had no past, where an old wall would be a sensation, and a tombstone of anybody's great grandfather the marvel of the whole region, the charms of the old world have an irresistible fascination. To visit the home of the Cæsars they have read of in their school books, and to look at architecture which they have seen pictorially, but have nothing like it in existence around them, is very naturally the strong wish of people who are nationally nomadic, and who have all more or less a smattering of education. Artemus Ward never expressed to me any very great wish to travel on the European continent, but to see London was to accomplish something which he had dreamed of from his boyhood. There runs from Marysville in California to Oroville in the same State a short and singular little railway, which, when we were there, was in a most unfinished condition. To Oroville we were going. We were too early for the train at the Marysville station, and sat down on a pile of timber to chat over future prospects.

"What sort of a man was Albert Smith?" asked Artemus, "And do you think that the Mormons would be as good a subject for the Londoners as Mont Blanc was?"

I answered his questions. He reflected for a few moments, and then said,

"Well, old fellow, I'll tell you what I should like to do.

I should like to go to London and give my lecture in the same place. Can it be done?"

It was done. Not in the same room, but under the same roof and on the same floor; in that gloomy-looking Hall in Piccadilly, which was destined to be the ante-chamber to the tomb of both lecturers.

Throughout this brief sketch I have written familiarly of the late Mr. Charles F. Browne as "Artemus Ward," or simply as "Artemus." I have done so advisedly, mainly because, during the whole course of our acquaintance, I do not remember addressing him as "Mr. Browne," or by his real Christian name. To me he was always "Artemus"— Artemus the kind, the gentle, the suave, the generous. One who was ever a friend in the fullest meaning of the word, and the best of companions in the amplest acceptance of the phrase. His merry laugh and pleasant conversation are as audible to me as if they were heard but yesterday; his words of kindness linger on the ear of memory, and his tones of genial mirth live in echoes which I shall listen to for evermore. Two years will soon have passed away since last he spoke, and—

> "Silence now, enamoured of his voice
> Locks its mute music in her rugged cell."

E. P. HINGSTON.

London,
October, 1868.

THE LECTURE.

A RTEMUS WARD'S first lecture in London was delivered at the Egyptian Hall, Piccadilly, on Tuesday, November 13, 1866. The room used was that which had been recently occupied by Mr. Arthur Sketchley. It is the lesser of the two rooms at the top of the staircase. Not the one in which Mr. Albert Smith formerly made his appearances. The attendance was very large, but the audience for the most part consisted of invited friends and the members of the press. The paying public having to wait for another opportunity, though they struggled in large numbers to obtain admission.

Copies of Artemus Ward's very original programmes are given in the Appendix, together with the notice of the lecture which appeared in the *Times* two days after its delivery. The notice was written by Mr. John Oxenford.

THE PROSCENIUM
WITH THE CURTAIN DOWN.

As at Artemus Ward's First Lecture in the Egyptian Hall, London, On Tuesday, November 13, 1866.

This was the appearance of the stage during the prologue of the lecture, before any portion of the panorama was exhibited. The lights in the room being then turned up, the wondrous gravity of the lecturer's face was fully visible at the time that he was uttering his best jokes. The picture was surrounded with a large gilt frame.

THE LECTURE.

By Artemus Ward.

YOU are entirely welcome ladies and gentlemen to my little picture-shop.[1]

I couldn't give you a very clear idea of the Mormons—and Utah—and the Plains—and the Rocky Mountains—without opening a picture-shop——and therefore I open one.

---

[1] "*My little picture-shop.*"—I have already stated that the room used was the lesser of the two on the first-floor of the Egyptian Hall. The panorama was to the left on entering, and Artemus Ward stood at the south-east corner facing the door. He had beside him a music-stand, on which for the first few days he availed himself of the assistance afforded by a sheet of foolscap on which all his "cues" were written out in a large hand. The proscenium was covered with dark

I don't expect to do great things here—but I have thought that if I could make money enough to buy me a passage to New Zealand[2] I should feel that I had not lived in vain.

I don't want to live in vain.——I'd rather live in Margate—or here. But

cloth, and the picture bounded by a great gilt frame. On the rostrum behind the lecturer was a little door giving admission to the space behind the picture where the piano was placed. Through this door Artemus would disappear occasionally in the course of the evening, either to instruct his pianist to play a few more bars of music, to tell his assistants to roll the picture more quickly or more slowly, or to give some instructions to the man who worked "the moon." The little lecture-room was thronged nightly during the very few weeks of its being open.

[2] "*To New Zealand.*"—Artemus Ward seriously contemplated a visit to Australia, after having made the tour of England. He was very much interested in all Australian affairs, had a strong desire to see the lands of the South, and looked forward to the long sea-voyage as one of the means by which he should regain his lost health.

I wish when the Egyptians built this hall they had given it a little more ventilation.³

If you should be dissatisfied with anything here to-night—I will admit you all free in New Zealand—if you will come to me there for the orders. Any respectable cannibal will tell you where I live. This shows that I have a forgiving spirit.

I really don't care for money. I only travel round to see the world and to exhibit my clothes. These clothes I have on were a great success in America.⁴

³ "*More ventilation.*"—The heat and closeness of the densely-packed room was a cause of common complaint among the audience.

⁴ "*These clothes, etc.*"—This was one of poor Artemus's jokes which owed more of its success to its oddity than to its veracity. While lecturing at the Egyptian Hall he wore a fashionably-cut dress coat in the evening. It was what he

How often do large fortunes ruin young men! I should like to be ruined, but I can get on very well as I am.

I am not an Artist. I don't paint myself—— though perhaps if I were a middle-aged single lady I should —— yet I have a passion for pictures.—— I have had a great many pictures—photographs— taken of myself. Some of them are very pretty —rather sweet to look at for a short time—and as I said before I like them. I've always loved pictures.

had never done during his lecture-career in the States, and he used privately to complain how uncomfortable he felt in it. He assumed the most deplorable look when pointing out his costume to his audience. His voice dropped into a moody reflective tone, and then suddenly passed into a much higher key when he commenced to allude to "large fortunes." He seemed to have shaken off the embarrassment of his fashionable clothes, and to be glad to pass on to another subject. In the punctuation of the succeeding paragraph of the lecture, I have endeavoured to convey an idea of the long pause he made between some of his sentences.

I could draw on wood at a very tender age. When a mere child I once drew a small cartload of raw turnips over a wooden bridge.——The people of the village noticed me. I drew their attention. They said I had a future before me. Up to that time I had an idea it was behind me.

Time passed on. It always does by the way. You may possibly have noticed that Time passes on.——It is a kind of way Time has.

I became a man. I haven't distinguished myself at all as an artist—but I have always been more or less mixed up with Art. I have an uncle who takes photographs—and I have a servant who——takes anything he can get his hands on.

When I was in Rome——Rome in New York State I mean——a distinguished sculpist wanted to sculp me. But I said "No." I saw through the designing man. My model once in his hands —he would have flooded the market with my busts——and I couldn't stand it to see everybody going round with a bust of me. Everybody would want one of course—and wherever I should go I should meet the educated classes with my bust, taking it home to their families. This would be more than my modesty could stand——and I should have to return to America————where my creditors are.

I like Art. I admire dramatic Art—although I failed as an actor.

It was in my schoolboy days that I failed as an actor.[5]———The play was the "Ruins of Pom-

---

[5] "*Failed as an actor.*"—Artemus made many attempts as an amateur actor, but never to his own satisfaction. He was very fond of the society of actors and actresses. Their weaknesses amused him as much as their talents excited his admiration. One of his favourite sayings was that the world was made up of "men, women, and the people on the stage."

peii."——I played the Ruins. It was not a very successful performance—but it was better than the "Burning Mountain." He was not good. He was a bad Vesuvius.

The remembrance often makes me ask—"Where are the boys of my youth?"——I assure you this is not a conundrum.——Some are amongst you here——some in America——some are in gaol.——

Hence arises a most touching question—"Where are the girls of my youth?" Some are married——some would like to be.

Oh my Maria! Alas! she married another. They frequently do. I hope she is happy—because I am.⁶——Some people are not happy. I have noticed that.

⁶ "*Because I am!*"—Spoken with a sigh. It was a joke which always told. Artemus never failed to use it in his "Babes in the Wood" lecture, and the "Sixty Minutes in Africa," as well as in the Mormon story.

A gentleman friend of mine came to me one day with tears in his eyes. I said "Why these weeps?" He said he had a mortgage on his farm—and wanted to borrow £200. I lent him the money—and he went away. Some time after he returned with more tears. He said he must leave me for ever. I ventured to remind him of the £200 he borrowed. He was much cut up. I thought I would not be hard upon him—so told him I would throw off one hundred pounds. He brightened—shook my hand—and said—"Old friend—I won't allow you to outdo me in liberality——I'll throw off the other hundred."

As a manager I was always rather more successful than as an actor.

Some years ago I engaged a celebrated Living American Skeleton for a tour through Australia.

He was the thinnest man I ever saw. He was a splendid skeleton. He didn't weigh anything scarcely——and I said to myself—the people of Australia will flock to see this tremendous curiosity. It is a long voyage—as you know—from New York to Melbourne—and to my utter surprise the skeleton had no sooner got out to sea than he commenced eating in the most horrible manner. He had never been on the ocean before—and he said it agreed with him.——I thought so!——I never saw a man eat so much in my life. Beef—mutton—pork——he swallowed them all like a shark———and between meals he was often discovered behind barrels eating hard-boiled eggs. The result was that when we reached Melbourne this infamous skeleton weighed 64 pounds more than I did!

I thought I was ruined——but I wasn't. I took him on to California——another very long sea voyage——and when I got him to San Francisco I exhibited him as a Fat Man.⁷

This story hasn't anything to do with my Entertainment, I know —— but one of the principal features of my Entertainment is that it contains so many things that don't have anything to do with it.

My Orchestra is small——but I am sure it is very good—so far as it goes. I give my pianist ten pounds a night—and his washing.⁸

---

⁷ "*As a Fat Man.*"—The reader need scarcely be informed that this narrative is about as real as "A. Ward's Snaiks," and about as much matter-of-fact as his journey through the States with a wax-work show.

⁸ "*My Pianist, &c.*" That a good pianist could be hired for a small sum in England was a matter of amusement to Artemus. More especially when he found a gentleman who was obliging enough to play anything he desired, such as break-downs and airs which had the most absurd relation to the scene they were used to illustrate. In the United States his pianist was desirous of playing music of a superior order, much against the consent of the lecturer.

I like Music.——I can't sing. As a singist I am not a success. I am saddest when I sing. So are those who hear me. They are sadder even than I am.

The other night some silver-voiced young men came under my window and sang—"Come where my love lies dreaming."——I didn't go. I didn't think it would be correct.

I found music very soothing when I lay ill with fever in Utah——and I was very ill——I was fearfully wasted.——My face was hewn down to nothing—and my nose was so sharp I didn't dare stick it into other people's business—for fear it would stay there—and I should never get it again. And on those dismal days a Mormon lady ——she was married—tho' not so much so as her husband—he had fifteen other wives——she used to sing a ballad commencing "Sweet bird—do not fly away!"——and I told her I wouldn't.——

She played the accordion divinely—accordionly I praised her.

I met a man in Oregon who hadn't any teeth—not a tooth in his head——yet that man could play on the bass drum better than any man I ever met.——He kept a hotel. They have queer hotels in Oregon. I remember one where they gave me a bag of oats for a pillow——I had night mares of course. In the morning the landlord said—How do you feel—old hoss—hay?——I told him I felt my oats.

[9]PERMIT me now to quietly state that altho' I am here with my cap and bells I am also here with some serious descriptions of the Mormons—their manners—their customs——and while the pictures I shall present to your notice are by no means works of art—they are painted from pho-

[9] "*Permit me now.*" Though the serious part of the lecture was here entered upon, it was not delivered in a graver tone than that in which he had spoken the farcicalities of the prologue. Most of the prefatory matter was given with an air of earnest thought; the arms sometimes folded, and the chin resting on one hand. On the occasion of his first exhibiting the panorama at New York he used a fishing-rod to point out the picture with; subsequently he availed himself of an old umbrella. In the Egyptian Hall he used his little riding-whip.

tographs actually taken on the spot[10]——and I am sure I need not inform any person present who was ever in the territory of Utah that they are as faithful as they could possibly be.[11]

I went to Great Salt Lake City by way of California.[12]

[10] "*Photographs.*" They were photographed by Savage and Ottinger, of Salt Lake City, the photographers to Brigham Young.

[11] *Curtain.* The picture was concealed from view during the first part of the lecture by a crimson curtain. This was drawn together or opened many times in the course of the lecture, and at odd points of the picture. I am not aware that Artemus himself could have explained why he caused the curtain to be drawn at one place and not at another. Probably he thought it to be one of his good jokes that it should shut in the picture just when there was no reason for its being used.

[12] "*By way of California.*" That is, he went by steamer from New York to Aspinwall, thence across the Isthmus of Panama by railway, and then from Panama to California by another steamboat. A journey which then occupied about three weeks.

One of the United States Mail line of Steamers from New York to Aspinwall. Being a supplemental boat only, its arrangements were none of the best.

I went to California on the steamer "Ariel."
——This is the steamer "Ariel."

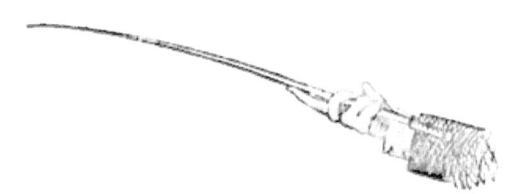

Oblige me by calmly gazing on the steamer "Ariel"——and when you go to California be sure and go on some other steamer—— because the "Ariel" isn't a very good one.

When I reached the "Ariel"—at pier No. 4 —New York—I found the passengers in a state of great confusion about their things—which were being thrown around by the ship's porters in a manner at once damaging and idiotic.——So great was the excitement—my fragile form was smashed this way—and jammed that way—till finally I was shoved into a stateroom which was occupied by two middle-aged females—who said "Base man—leave us—O, leave us!"——I left them ——Oh—I left them!

We reach Accapulco on the coast of Mexico in due time. Nothing of special interest occurred at Accapulco——only some of the Mexican ladies are very beautiful. They all have brilliant black hair——hair "black as starless night"——if I may quote from the "Family Herald." It don't curl.——A Mexican lady's hair never curls ———it is straight as an Indian's. Some people's hair won't curl under any circumstances. ——My hair won't curl under two shillings.[13]

---

[13] "*Under Two Shillings.*" Artemus always wore his hair straight until after his severe illness in Salt Lake City. So much of it dropped off during his recovery that he became dissatisfied with the long meagre appearance his countenance presented when he surveyed it in the looking-glass. After his lecture at the Salt Lake City Theatre he did not lecture again

MONTGOMERY STREET, SAN FRANCISCO.

The main street of the chief city of California. It is built over what was a few years ago a portion of the Bay of San Francisco. In digging up a part of the street, some time since, the excavators came upon the hull of an old vessel full of chests of tea. The Chinaman in the foreground was pointed out by the lecturer preparatory to his remarks on the Chinese theatre.

The great thoroughfare of the imperial city of the Pacific Coast.

The Chinese form a large element in the population of San Francisco — and I went to the Chinese Theatre.

until we had crossed the Rocky Mountains and arrived at Denver City, the capital of Colorado. On the afternoon he was to lecture there I met him coming out of an ironmonger's store with a small parcel in his hand. "I want you, old fellow," he said, "I have been all round the City for them, and I've got them at last." "Got what?" I asked. "A pair of curling-tongs. I am going to have my hair curled to lecture in to-night. I mean to cross the plains in curls. Come home with me and try to curl it for me. I don't want to go to any idiot of a barber to be laughed at." I played the part of *friseur*. Subsequently he became his own "curlist," as he phrased it. From that day forth Artemus was a curly-haired man.

A Chinese play often lasts two months. Commencing at the hero's birth, it is cheerfully conducted from week to week till he is either killed or married.

The night I was there a Chinese comic vocalist sang a Chinese comic song. It took him six weeks to finish it——but as my time was limited I went away at the expiration of 215 verses. There were 11,000 verses to this song — the chorus being "Tural lural dural, ri fol day"——which was repeated twice at the end of each verse ——making——as you will at once see——the appalling number of 22,000 "tural lural dural, ri fol days"——and the man still lives.

When Artemus Ward paid his visit here, there was a population of about 15,000, with three daily newspapers. Five years previously it had no existence. It was the largest place between the Sierra Nevada Mountains and Salt Lake City. (1863.)

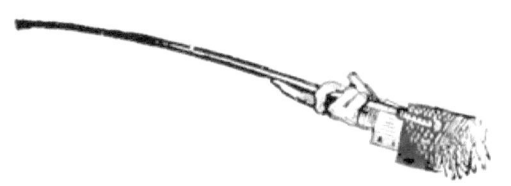

Virginia City—in the bright new State of Nevada.[14]

A wonderful little city—right in the heart of the famous Washoe silver regions —— the mines of which annually produce over twenty-five millions of solid silver. This silver is melted into solid bricks—of about the size of ordinary

[14] "*Virginia City.*" The view of Virginia City given in the panorama conveyed a very poor idea of the marvellous capital of the silver region of Nevada. Artemus caused the curtain to close up between his view of San Francisco and that of Virginia City, as a simple means of conveying an idea of the distance travelled between. To arrive at the city of silver we had to travel from San Francisco to Sacramento by steamboat, thence from Sacramento to Folsom by railroad, then by coach to Placerville. At Placerville we commenced the ascent of the Sierra Nevada, gaining the summit of Johnson's Pass about

house-bricks—and carted off to San Francisco with mules. The roads often swarm with these silver wagons.

One hundred and seventy-five miles to the east of this place are the Reese River Silver Mines—which are supposed to be the richest in the world.

four o'clock in the morning; thence we descended; skirted the shores of Lake Tahoe, and arrived at Carson City, where Artemus lectured. From Carson, the next trip was across an arid plain, to the great silver region. Empire City, the first place we struck, was composed of about fifty wooden houses and three or four quartz mills. Leaving it behind us, we passed through the Devil's Gate—a grand ravine, with precipitous mountains on each side; then we came to Silver City, Gold Hill, and Virginia. The road was all up-hill. Virginia City itself is built on a ledge cut out of the side of Mount Davidson, which rises some 9,000 feet above the sea level—the city being about half way up its side. To Artemus Ward the wild character of the scenery, the strange manners of the red-shirted citizens, and the odd developments of life met with in that uncouth mountain-town were all replete with

Herbage on the plains of Nevada consists almost exclusively of the Sage-brush (Artemisia tridentata), the most dreary-looking of shrubs. The leaves are of a leaden colour, and the stems are gnarled and wiry.

The great American Desert in winter-time——the desert which is so frightfully gloomy always. No trees——no houses——no people—save the miserable beings who live in wretched huts and have charge of the horses and mules of the Overland Mail Company.

interest. We stayed there about a week. During the time of our stay he explored every part of the place, met many old friends from the Eastern States, and formed many new acquaintances, with some of whom acquaintance ripened into warm friendship. Among the latter was Mr. Samuel L. Clemens, now well known as "Mark Twain." He was then sub-editing one of the three papers published daily in Virginia—*The Territorial Enterprise*. Artemus detected in the writings of Mark Twain the indications of great humorous power, and strongly advised the writer to seek a better field

This picture is a great work of art.——It is an oil painting—done in petroleum. It is by the Old Masters. It was the last thing they did before dying. They did this and then they expired.

for his talents. Since then he has become a well-known New York lecturer and author. With Mark Twain, Artemus made a descent into the Gould and Curry Silver Mine at Virginia, the largest mine of the kind, I believe, in the world. The account of the descent formed a long and very amusing article in the next morning's *Enterprise*. To wander about the town and note its strange developments occupied Artemus incessantly. I was sitting writing letters at the hotel when he came in hurriedly, and requested me to go out with him. "Come and see some joking much better than mine," said he. He led me to where one of Wells, Fargo, & Co.'s express waggons was being rapidly filled with silver bricks. Ingots of the precious metal, each almost as large as an ordinary brick, were being thrown from one man to another to load the waggon, just as bricks or cheeses are transferred from hand to had by carters in England. "Good old jokes those, Hingston. Good, solid 'Babes in the Wood,'" observed Artemus. Yet that evening he lectured in "Maguire's Opera House," Virginia City, to an audience composed chiefly of

The most celebrated artists of London are so delighted with this picture that they come to the Hall every day to gaze at it. I wish you were nearer to it—so you could see it better. I wish I could take it to your residences and let you see

miners, and the receipts were not far short of eight hundred dollars. A droll building it was to be called an "Opera House," and to bear that designation in a place so outlandish. Perched up on the side of a mountain—from the windows of the dressing rooms—a view could be had of fifty miles of the American desert. It was an "Opera House;" yet in the plain beneath it there were Indians who still led the life of savages, and carried dried human scalps attached to their girdles. It was an "Opera House;" yet, for many hundred miles around it, Nature wore the roughest, sternest, and most barren of aspects—no tree, no grass, no shrub, but the colourless and dreary sage-brush. Every piece of timber, every brick, and every stone in that "Opera House" had been brought from California, over those snow-capped *Sierras*, which, but a few years before had been regarded as beyond the last outposts of civilisation. Every singer who had sung, and every actor who had performed at that "Opera House" had been whirled down the sides of the Nevada mountains, clinging to the coach-top, and mentally vowing never

it by daylight. Some of the greatest artists in London come here every morning before daylight with lanterns to look at. They say they never saw anything like it before——and they hope they never shall again.

again to trust the safety of his neck on any such professional excursion. The drama has been very plucky "out West." Thalia, Melpomene, and Euterpe become young ladies of great animal spirits, and fearless daring, when they feel the fresh breezes of the Pacific blowing in their faces. At Virginia City we purchased black felt shirts half an inch thick, and grey blankets of ample size to keep us warm for the journey we were about to undertake. We invested also in revolvers to defend ourselves against the Indians; a dozen cold roast fowls to eat on the way; a demijohn of Bourbon whisky, and a bagful of unground coffee. This last was about as useful as any of our purchases. Thus provided, we started across the desert on our way to Reese River, and thence to Salt Lake City. Our coach was a fearfully lumbering old vehicle of great strength, constructed for jolting over rocky ledges, plunging into marshy swamps, and for rolling through miles of sand. The horses were small and wiry, accustomed to the country, and able to exist on anything

When I first showed this picture in New York, the audience were so enthusiastic in their admiration of this picture that they called for the Artist———and when he appeared they threw brickbats at him."[11*]

which it is possible for a horse to eat. There were four of us in the coach. The "Pioneer Company's" man who drove us was full of whisky and good-humour when he mounted the box, and singing in chorus, "Jordan's a hard road to travel on," we bowled down the slope of Mount Davidson towards the deserts of Nevada, *en route* for New Pass Station.

[11*] "*Threw brickbats at him.*" This portion of the panorama was very badly painted. When the idea of having a panorama was first entertained by Artemus he wished to have one of great artistic merit. Finding considerable difficulty in procuring one, and also discovering that the expense of a real work of art would be beyond his means, he resolved on having a very bad one, or one so bad in parts that its very badness would give him scope for jest. In the small towns of the Western States it passed very well for a first-class picture, but what it was really worth in an artistic point of view its owner was very well aware.

A bird's-eye-view of Great Salt Lake City ———— the strange city in the Desert about which so much has been heard———— the city of the people who call themselves Saints.[15]

I know there is much interest taken in these remarkable people—ladies and gentlemen————and

---

[15] "*Salt Lake City.*" Our stay in the Mormon capital extended over six weeks. So cheerless was the place in midwinter, that we should not have stayed half that time had not Artemus Ward succumbed to an attack of typhoid fever almost as soon as we arrived. The incessant travel by night and day, the depressing effect produced by intense cold, travelling through leagues of snow and fording half-frozen rivers at midnight, the excitement of passing through Indian country, and some slight nervous apprehension of how he

The City is laid out in squares; each house standing on an acre and a quarter of ground, with a canal of clear water flowing in front. (This picture joins on the one which follows it.)

FROM THE HEIGHTS BEHIND IT.

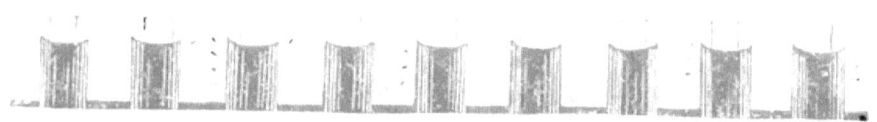

The building in the foreground is the Mormon arsenal. To the right, in the mid-distance, is the River Jordan, flowing from Lake Utah to the Salt Lake. The valley through which the Jordan flows is one of the most fertile on the North American continent.

I have thought it better to make the purely descriptive part of my Entertainment entirely serious.———I will not—then—for the next ten minutes—confine myself to my subject.

Some seventeen years ago a small band of Mormons—headed by Brigham Young—commenced in the present thrifty metropolis of Utah. The population of the territory of Utah is over 100,000—chiefly Mormons——and they are increasing at the rate of from five to ten thousand

would be received among the Mormons, considering that he had ridiculed them in a paper published some time before, all conspired to produce the illness which resulted. Fever of the typhoid form is not uncommon in Utah. Probably the rarefaction of the air on a plateau 4,000 feet above the sea level has something to do with its frequency. Artemus's fears relative to the cordiality of his reception proved to be groundless, for during the period of his being ill he was carefully tended. Brigham Young commissioned Mr. Sten-

annually. The converts to Mormonism now are almost exclusively confined to English and Germans.——Wales and Cornwall have contributed largely to the population of Utah during the last few years. The population of Great Salt Lake City is 20,000.——The streets are eight

house, postmaster to the city and Elder of the Mormon Church, to visit him frequently and supply him with whatever he required. One of the two wives of Mr. Townsend, landlord of the Salt Lake House, the hotel where we stopped was equally as kind. Whatever the feelings of the Mormons were towards poor Artemus, they at least treated him with sympathetic hospitality. Even Mr. Porter Rockwell, who is known as one of the "Avenging Angels," or "Danite Band," and who is reported to have made away with some seventeen or eighteen enemies of the "Saints," came and sat by the bedside of the sufferer, detailing to him some of the little "difficulties" he had experienced in effectually silencing the unbelievers of times past.

rods wide*—and are neither flagged nor paved. A stream of pure mountain spring water courses through each street—and is conducted into the Gardens of the Mormons. The houses are mostly of adobe—or sun-dried brick—and present a neat and comfortable appearance.——They are usually a story and a half high. Now and then you see a fine modern house in Salt Lake City——but no house that is dirty, shabby, and dilapidated—because there are no absolutely poor people in Utah. Every Mormon has a nice garden——and every Mormon has a tidy dooryard.—— Neatness is a great characteristic of the Mormons.

The Mormons profess to believe that they are the chosen people of God———they call themselves Latter-day Saints——and they call us people of the outer world Gentiles. They say

* Equal to 64 feet wide.

that Mr. Brigham Young is a prophet—the legitimate successor of Joseph Smith—who founded the Mormon religion. They also say they are authorised—by special revelation from Heaven—to marry as many wives as they can comfortably support.

This wife-system they call plurality——the world calls it polygamy. That at its best it is an accursed thing—I need not of course inform you ——but you will bear in mind that I am here as a rather cheerful reporter of what I saw in Utah——and I fancy it isn't at all necessary for me to grow virtuously indignant over something we all know is hideously wrong.

You will be surprised to hear—I was amazed to see—that among the Mormon women there are some few persons of education—of positive cultivation. As a class the Mormons are not an educated people——but they are by no means the community of ignoramuses so many writers have told us they were.

The valley in which they live is splendidly favoured. They raise immense crops. They have mills of all kinds. They have coal—lead—and silver mines. All they eat—all they drink—all they wear they can produce themselves—and still have a great abundance to sell to the gold regions of Idaho on the one hand—and the silver regions of Nevada on the other.

The President of this remarkable community——the head of the Mormon Church——is Brigham Young.———He is called President Young—and Brother Brigham. He is about 54 years old—altho' he doesn't look to be over 45. He has sandy hair and whiskers——is of medium height——and is a little inclined to corpulency.

He was born in the State of Vermont. His power is more absolute than that of any living sovereign——yet he uses it with such consummate discretion that his people are almost madly devoted to him—and that they would cheerfully die for him if they thought the sacrifice were demanded—I cannot doubt.

He is a man of enormous wealth.——One-tenth of everything sold in the territory of Utah goes to the Church——and Mr. Brigham Young is the Church. It is supposed that he speculates with these funds————at all events—he is one of the wealthiest men now living——worth several millions—without doubt.——He is a bold—bad man——but that he is also a man of extraordinary administrative ability no one can doubt who has watched his astounding career for the past ten years. It is only fair for me to add that he treated me with marked kindness during my sojourn in Utah.

The hotel in Salt Lake City at which Artemus Ward stopped during his six weeks' stay, and where he was seized with illness. In the distance are the Wahsatch Mountains.

The West Side of Main Street—Salt Lake City —including a view of the Salt Lake Hotel.——It is a temperance hotel.[16] I prefer temperance hotels—altho' they sell worse liquor than

---

[16] "*Temperance Hotel.*" At the date of our visit, there was only one place in Salt Lake City where strong drink was allowed to be sold. Brigham Young himself owned the property, and vended the liquor by wholesale, not permitting any of it to be drunk on the premises. It was a coarse, inferior kind of whisky, known in Salt Lake as "Valley Tan." Throughout the city there was no drinking-bar nor billiard room, so far as I am aware. But a drink on the sly could always be had at one of the hard-goods stores, in the back office behind the pile of metal saucepans; or at one of the

any other kind of hotels. But the Salt Lake Hotel sells none———nor is there a bar in all Salt Lake City——but I found when I was thirsty —and I generally am—that I could get some very good brandy of one of the Elders—on the sly—and I never on any account allow my business to interfere with my drinking.

dry-goods stores, in the little parlour in the rear of the bales of calico. At the present time I believe that there are two or three open bars in Salt Lake, Brigham Young having recognised the right of the "Saints" to "liquor up" occasionally. But whatever other failings they may have, intemperance cannot be laid to their charge. Among the Mormons there are no paupers, no gamblers, and no drunkards.

This picture is a continuation of the preceding one. The room in which Artemus resided was that in the white part of the house, under the Verandah. The hotel was kept by Mr. James Townsend, a Mormon.

In the panorama, the Coach is made a much more sightly object than it really was. Instead of looking like a respectable omnibus, it was a huge jolting affair of cumbrous proportions, with sad arrangements for internal comfort.

There is the Overland Mail Coach.[17]——That is, the den on wheels in which we have been

[17] "*Overland Mail Coach.*" From Virginia City to Salt Lake we travelled in the coaches of the "Pioneer Stage Company." In leaving Salt Lake for Denver we changed to those of the "Overland Stage Company," of which the renowned Ben Holliday is proprietor, a gentleman whose name on the Plains is better known than that of any other man in America.

crammed for the past ten days—and ten nights.
———Those of you who have been in Newgate[18]—

——— ——— ——— ——— ——— ——— ——— —— ——

——— ——— ——— ——— ——— ——— ———

and staid there any length of time———as
visitors———can realize how I felt.

[18] "*Been in Newgate.*" The manner in which Artemus uttered this joke was peculiarly characteristic of his style of lecturing. The commencement of the sentence was spoken as if unpremeditated; then, when he had got as far as the word "Newgate," he paused, as if wishing to call back that which he had said. The applause was unfailingly uproarious. Travelling through the States, he used to say, "Those of you who have been in the Penitentiary." On the morning after his lecture at Pittsburg in Pennsylvania, he was waited on by a tall, gaunt, dark-haired man, of sour aspect and sombre demeanour, who carried in his hand a hickory walking-cane, which he grasped very menacingly, as addressing Artemus he said, "I guess you are the gentleman who lect'red last night?" Mr. Ward replied in the affirmative. "Then I've

The American Overland Mail Route commences at Sacramento—California——and ends at Atchison—Kansas. The distance is two thousand two hundred miles——but you go part

got to have satisfaction from you. I took my wife and her sister to hear you lecter, and you insulted them." "Excuse me," said Artemus. "I went home immediately the lecture was over, and had no conversation with any lady in the hall that evening." The visitor grew more angry, "Hold thar, Mr. Lect'rer. You told my wife and her sister that they'd been in the Penitentiary. I must have satisfaction for the insult, and I'm come to get it." Artemus was hesitating how to reply, when the hotel clerk suddenly appeared upon the scene, saying, "I've a good memory for voices. You are Mr. Josiah Mertin, I believe?" "I am," was the reply. "And I am the late clerk of the Girard House, Philadelphia. There's a little board-bill of yours owing there for ninety-two dollars and a half. You skedaddled without paying. Will you oblige me by waiting till I send for an officer?" I believe that Mr. Josiah Mertin did not even wait for "satisfaction."

of the way by rail. The Pacific Railway[19] is now completed from Sacramento — California — to Fulsom — California —— which only leaves two thousand two hundred and eleven miles to go by coach. This breaks the monotony———it came very near breaking my back.

[19] "*The Pacific Railway.*" The journey was made in the winter of 1863-4. By the time these notes appear in print, the Pacific Railway will be almost complete from the banks of the Missouri to those of the Sacramento, and travellers will soon be able to make the transit of over three thousand miles from New York City to the capital of California, without leaving the railway car, except to cross a ferry, or to change from one station to another.

A brief description of this building will be found in the notes appended to the lecture. Artemus Ward lectured here on "The Babes in the Wood." It was built by Brigham Young, and is his property.

The Mormon Theatre.——This edifice is the exclusive property of Brigham Young. It will comfortably hold 3,000 persons—and I beg you will believe me when I inform you that its interior is quite as brilliant as that of any theatre in London.[20]

[20] "*Brilliant as that of any theatre in London.*" Herein Artemus slightly exaggerated. The colouring of the theatre was white and gold, but it was inefficiently lighted with oil lamps. When Brigham Young himself showed us round the theatre, he pointed out, as an instance of his own ingenuity, that the central chandelier was formed out of the wheel of one of his old coaches. The house is now, I believe, lighted with gas. Altogether it is a very wondrous edifice, considering where it is built and who were the builders. At the time of its erection there was no other theatre on the northern

The actors are all Mormon amateurs, who charge nothing for their services.

You must know that very little money is taken at the doors of this theatre. The Mormons mostly pay in grain—and all sorts of articles.

The night I gave my little lecture there—among my receipts were corn—flour—pork—

part of the American plateau, no building for a similar purpose anywhere for five hundred miles, north, east, south, or west. Many a theatre in the provincial towns of England is not half so substantially built, nor one tithe-part so well appointed. The dressing rooms, wardrobe, tailors' workshop, carpenters' shop, paint room, and library, leave scarcely anything to be desired in their completeness. Brigham Young's son-in-law, Mr. Hiram Clawson, the manager, and Mr. John Cane, the stage manager, if they came to London, might render good service at one or two of our metropolitan playhouses.

cheese—chickens —— on foot and in the shell.

One family went in on a live pig —— and a man attempted to pass a "yaller dog" at the Box Office—but my agent repulsed him. One offered me a doll for admission —— another infants' clothing. —— I refused to take that. —— As a general rule I do refuse.

In the middle of the parquet—in a rocking chair—with his hat on—sits Brigham Young. When the play drags—he either goes out or falls into a tranquil sleep.

A portion of the dress-circle is set apart for the wives of Brigham Young. From ten to twenty of them are usually present. His children fill the entire gallery—and more too.

The East Side of Main Street—Salt Lake City—with a view of the Council Building.—— The legislature of Utah meets there. It is like all legislative bodies. They meet this winter to repeal the laws which they met and made last winter——and they will meet next winter to repeal the laws which they met and made this winter.

I dislike to speak about it——but it was in Utah that I made the great speech of my life. I wish you could have heard it. I have a fine education. You may have noticed it. I speak six different languages —— London — Chatham—and Dover——Margate—Brighton—

The building to the extreme right is the House of Legislature, where the representatives of the territory of Utah hold their meetings. The second house on the right is the Post Office. Main Street is 132 feet in breadth.

and Hastings. My parents sold a cow—and sent me to college when I was quite young. During the vacation I used to teach a school of whales— and there's where I learned to spout.——I don't expect applause for a little thing like that. I wish you could have heard that speech—however. If Cicero——he's dead now——he has gone from us ———but if Old Ciss[21] could have heard that effort it would have given him the rinderpest. I'll tell you how it was. There are stationed in Utah two regiments of U. S. troops——the 21st from California—and the 37th from Nevada. The 20-onesters asked me to present a stand of colours

[21] "*Old Ciss.*" Here again no description can adequately inform the reader of the drollery which characterized the lecturer. His reference to Cicero was made in the most lugubrious manner, as if he really deplored his death and valued him as a schoolfellow loved and lost.

to the 37-sters——and I did it in a speech so
abounding in eloquence of a bold and brilliant
character——and also some sweet talk———real
pretty shop-keeping talk——that I worked the
enthusiasm of those soldiers up to such a
pitch—that they came very near shooting me on the spot.²²

²² "*United States Troops.*" Our stay in Utah was rendered especially pleasant by the attentions of the regiment of California Cavalry, then stationed at Fort Douglas in the Wahsatch Mountains, three miles beyond and overlooking the city. General Edward O'Connor, the United States Military Governor of Utah, was especially attentive to the wants of poor Artemus during his severe illness; and had it not been for the kind attentions of Dr. Williams, the surgeon to the regiment, I doubt if the invalid would have recovered. General O'Connor had then been two years stationed in Utah, but during the whole of that time had refused to have any personal communication with Brigham Young. The Mormon prophet would sit in his private box, and the United States general occupy a seat in the dress-circle of the theatre. They would look at each other frequently through their opera-glasses, but that constituted their whole intimacy.

This picture is a continuation of the preceding one. On the left is a portion of the enclosure wherein the new temple is being built. On the right part of the grounds belonging to the second in command in the Mormon Church—Mr. Heber C. Kimball.

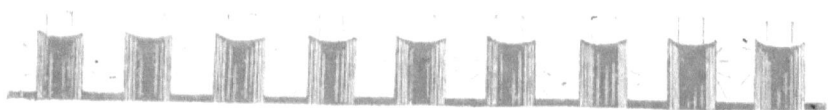

To the extreme left is the Lion House. (There is a lion over one of the windows.) It is the harem of the prophet. Every "wife" who inhabits it has a room similarly furnished. They meet in common on the verandah. Brigham Young himself lives with his favourite in the large middle house. The building with the tower to it on the right is the school-house, for the education of the prophet's children only.

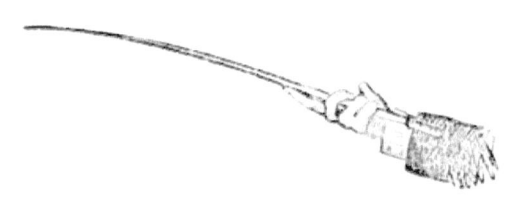

Brigham Young's Harem.——These are the houses of Brigham Young. The first on the right is the Lion House—so called because a crouching stone lion adorns the central front window. The adjoining small building is Brigham Young's office—and where he receives his visitors. ——The large house in the centre of the picture —which displays a huge bee-hive—is called the Bee House——the bee-hive is supposed to be symbolical of the industry of the Mormons.—— Mrs. Brigham Young the first—now quite an old lady—lives here with her children. None of the other wives of the prophet live here. In the rear are the school houses where Brigham Young's children are educated.

Brigham Young has two hundred wives. Just think of that! Oblige me by thinking of that. That is—he has eighty actual wives, and he is spiritually married to one hundred and twenty more. These spiritual marriages————as the Mormons call them————are contracted with aged widows—who think it a great honour to be sealed————the Mormons call it being sealed———— to the Prophet.

So we may say he has two hundred wives. He loves not wisely—but two hundred well. He is dreadfully married. He's the most married man I ever saw in my life.

I saw his mother-in-law while I was there. I can't exactly tell you how many there is of her—but it's a good deal. It strikes me that one mother-in-law is about enough to have in a family——unless you're very fond of excitement.

A few days before my arrival in Utah—Brigham was married again—to a young and really pretty girl²³——but he says he shall stop now. He told me confidentially that he shouldn't get married any more. He says that all he wants now is to live in peace for the remainder of his days—and have his dying pillow soothed by the loving hands of his family. Well—that's all right——that's all right—I suppose———but if *all* his family soothe his dying pillow—he'll have to go out-doors to die.

By the way—Shakespeare endorses polygamy.——He speaks of the Merry Wives of Windsor. How many wives did Mr. Windsor have?——But we will let this pass.

[23] "*A really pretty Girl.*" The daughter of the architect of his new theatre.

Some of these Mormons have terrific families. I lectured one night by invitation in the Mormon village of Provost——but during the day I rashly gave a leading Mormon an order admitting himself and family.——It was before I knew that he was much married——and they filled the room to overflowing. It was a great success ——but I didn't get any money.

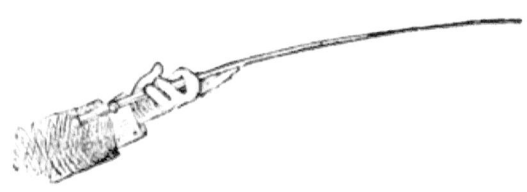

Heber C. Kimball's Harem. —— Mr. C. Kimball is the first vice-president of the Mormon church—and would—consequently—succeed to the full presidency on Brigham Young's death.

Brother Kimball is a gay and festive cuss of some seventy summers——or some'ers there

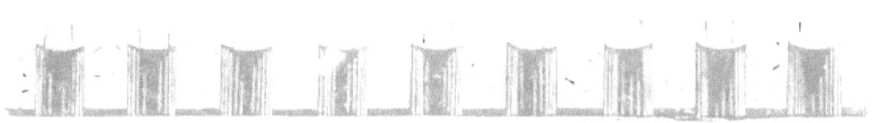

The seraglio of Mr. Kimball is large. Unlike Brigham Young, he does not keep his wives under one roof, but has many buildings in his garden, where he assorts them according to their temper and their adaptability to dwelling together in peace.

He says they are awful eaters.

Mr. Kimball had a son——a lovely young man——who was married to ten interesting wives. But one day——while he was absent from home——these ten wives went out walking with a handsome young man—which so enraged Mr. Kimball's son—which made Mr. Kimball's son so jealous—that he shot himself with a horse pistuel.

[21] "*A hundred head of Wives.*" It is an authenticated fact that, in an address to his congregation in the tabernacle, Heber C. Kimball once alluded to his wives by the endearing epithet of "my heifers;" and on another occasion politely spoke of them as "his cows." The phraseology may possibly be a slight indication of the refinement of manners prevalent in Salt Lake City.

The doctor who attended him——a very scientific man—— informed me that the bullet entered the inner parallelogram of his diaphragmatic thorax, superinducing membranous hemorrhage in the outer cuticle of his basilicon-thamaturgist. It killed him. I should have thought it would.

(Soft music.)[25]

I hope his sad end will be a warning to all young wives who go out walking with handsome young men. Mr. Kimball's son is now

---

[25] "*Soft Music.*" Here Artemus Ward's pianist (following instructions) sometimes played the dead march from "*Saul.*" At other times, the Welsh air of "Poor Mary Anne;" or anything else replete with sadness which might chance to strike his fancy. The effect was irresistibly comic.

no more. He sleeps beneath the cypress—the myrtle—and the willow. This music is a dirge by the eminent pianist for Mr. Kimball's son. He died by request.

I regret to say that efforts were made to make a Mormon of me while I was in Utah.

It was leap-year when I was there—and seventeen young widows——the wives of a deceased Mormon——offered me their hearts and hands. I called on them one day—and taking their soft white hands in mine——which made eighteen hands altogether——I found them in tears.

And I said—"Why is this thus? What is the reason of this thusness?"

They hove a sigh——seventeen sighs of different sizes.——They said—

"Oh—soon thou wilt be gonested away!"

I told them that when I got ready to leave a place I wentested.

They said—"Doth not like us?"

I said—"I doth——I doth!"

I also said—"I hope your intentions are honourable—as I am a lone child——my parent being far—far away.

They then said—"Wilt not marry us?"

I said—"Oh—no——it cannot was."

Again they asked me to marry them—and again I declined. When they cried—

TABERNACLE AND BOWERY.

The Tabernacle is the building to the left; to the right of it, and within the same enclosure, is the Bowery: a large shed with boughs of trees laid over it, the sides being open. In it religious services are held during the summer months.

"Oh—cruel man! This is too much——oh! too much!"

I told them that it was on account of the muchness that I declined.[26]

This is the Mormon Temple.

It is built of adobe—and will hold five thousand persons quite comfortably. A full brass and

---

[26] "*That I declined.*" I remember one evening party in Salt Lake City to which Artemus Ward and myself went. There were thirty-nine ladies and only seven gentlemen.

string band often assists the choir of this church ——and the choir—I may add—is a remarkably good one.

Brigham Young seldom preaches now. The younger elders——unless on some special occasion——conduct the services. I only heard Mr. Young once. He is not an educated man——but speaks with considerable force and clearness. The day I was there there was nothing coarse in his remarks.

The foundations of the Temple.

These are the foundations of the magnificent Temple the Mormons are building. It is to be

From this picture and that which succeeds may be formed some idea of how far the building of the New Temple had progressed at the time of the lecturer's visit. The stones were being shaped into form by masons who contributed their labour gratuitously.

CONTINUED.

The block is forty rods square, and contains ten acres. The position is 4,300 feet above the level of the sea in latitude 40° 45' 44" N., and longitude 112° 6' 8" W. of Greenwich.

built of hewn stone—and will cover several acres of ground. They say it shall eclipse in splendour all other temples in the world. They also say it shall be paved with solid gold.*

It is perhaps worthy of remark that the architect of this contemplated gorgeous affair repudiated Mormonism—and is now living in London.

---

* "*Solid Gold.*" "Where will the gold be obtained from?" is a question which the visitor might reasonably be expected to ask. Unquestionably the mountains of Utah contain the precious metal, though it has not been the policy of Brigham Young and the chiefs of the Mormon Church to disclose their knowledge of the localities in which it is to be found. There is a current report in Salt Lake City that nuggets of gold have been picked up within a radius of a few score of miles from the site of the new temple. But the Mormons, instructed by their Church, profess ignorance on the subject. The discovery of large gold mines, and permission to work them, would attract to the valley of Salt Lake a class of visitors not wished for by Brigham Young and his disciples. Next to the construction of the Pacific Railway, nothing would be more conducive to the downfall of Mormonism than Utah becoming known as an extensive gold-field.

The Temple as it is to be.

This pretty little picture is from the architect's design——and cannot therefore—I suppose—be called a fancy sketch.[27]

Should the Mormons continue unmolested—I think they will complete this rather remarkable edifice.

[27] "*A Fancy Sketch.*" Artemus had the windows of the temple in his panorama cut out and filled in with transparent coloured paper, so that, when lighted from behind, it had the effect of one of the little plaster churches with a piece of lighted candle inside, which the Italian image-boys display at times for sale in the streets. Nothing in the course of the evening pleased Artemus more than to notice the satisfaction with which this meretricious piece of absurdity was received by the audience.

The view is copied from the original drawing by Mr. Truman O. Angell, the architect. There is very little chance under present circumstances that the Temple will be completed. The formation of the Pacific Railway will, in all probability, cause the Mormons to seek a home elsewhere.

It is situated in the north-eastern corner of Utah Territory to the north-west of the valley of Salt Lake and about eighteen miles from the city. Its length is nearly seventy miles; its breadth from thirty to thirty-five miles. (N.B. This is the moon in the management of which Artemus Ward's "moonist" was apt to experience difficulty.)

Great Salt Lake.——The great salt dead sea of the desert.

I know of no greater curiosity than this inland sea of thick brine. It is eighty miles wide—and one hundred and thirty miles long. Solid masses of salt are daily washed ashore in immense heaps —and the Mormon in want of salt has only to go to the shore of this lake and fill his cart. Only— the salt for table use has to be subjected to a boiling process.[2*]

[2* "*The Great Salt Lake.*" A very general mistake prevails among those not better informed that the Mormon capital is built upon the borders of the Salt Lake. There are eighteen miles of distance between them. Not from any part of the

These are facts—susceptible of the clearest possible proof. They tell one story about this lake—however—that I have my doubts about. They say a Mormon farmer drove forty head of cattle in there once—and they came out first-rate pickled beef.———

* * * * *
* * * * *
* * * * *
* * * * *
* * * * *

City proper can a view of the Lake be obtained. To get a glimpse of it without journeying towards it, the traveller must ascend to one of the rocky ledges in the range of mountains which back the city. So saline is the water of the lake, that three pailsful of it are said to yield on evaporation one pailful of salt. I never saw the experiment tried.

PRECEDING VIEW CONTINUED.

This Dead Sea of the Western world is supplied with fresh water from three rivers—the Bear River, the Weber, and the Jordan. The water, according to Captain Burton's statement, contains six times and a half more solid matter than the average solid constituents of sea water.

At this part of the entertainment the lights in the room were turned up, and the audience allowed a very brief "interval for refreshments." Artemus Ward had to recover from the fatigue of attending to the moon.

I sincerely hope you will excuse my absence——I am a man short—and have to work the moon myself.*

I shall be most happy to pay a good salary to any respectable boy of good parentage and education who is a good moonist.

* "*The Moon myself.*" Here Artemus would leave the rostrum for a few moments, and pretend to be engaged behind. The picture was painted for a night-scene, and the effect intended to be produced was that of the moon rising over the lake and rippling on the waters. It was produced in the usual dioramic way, by making the track of the moon transparent and throwing the moon on from the bull's eye of a lantern. When Artemus went behind, the moon would become nervous and flickering, dancing up and down in the most inartistic and undecided manner. The result was that, coupled with the lecturer's oddly expressed apology, the "moon" became one of the best laughed-at parts of the entertainment.

The Endowment House.[30]

In this building the Mormon is initiated into the mysteries of the faith.

Strange stories are told of the proceedings which are held in this building——but I have no possible means of knowing how true they may be.

---

[30] "*The Endowment House.*" To the young ladies of Utah this edifice possesses extreme interest. The Mormon ceremony of marriage is said to be of the most extraordinary character; various symbolical scenes being enacted, and the bride and bridegroom invested with sacred garments which they are never to part with. In all Salt Lake I could not find a person who would describe to me the ceremonies of the Endowment House, nor could Artemus or myself obtain admission within its mystic walls.

That which takes place within this building travellers may guess at but are not permitted to know. It is where the Mormon marriages are celebrated. On the mountain above a figure out of all proportion to the scenery is supposed to represent Artemus Ward attacked by a bear in front and a pack of wolves in the rear.

High bluffs of yellow colour and conglomerate formation, full of small fossils. The buildings at the base constitute Weber's Station, where the coach stops for the mules to be changed, and the passengers to obtain refreshments.

Echo Canyon.

Salt Lake City is fifty-five miles behind us—and this is Echo Canyon—in reaching which we are supposed to have crossed the summit of the Wahsatch Mountains. These ochre-coloured bluffs————formed of conglomerate sandstone—and full of fossils————signal the entrance to the Canyon. At its base lies Weber Station.

Echo Canyon is about twenty-five miles long. It is really the sublimest thing between the Missouri and the Sierra Nevada. The red wall to the left develops further up the Canyon into pyramids—buttresses—and castles——honey combed and fretted in nature's own massive magnificence of architecture.

In 1856—Echo Canyon was the place selected by Brigham Young for the Mormon General Wells to fortify and make impregnable against the advance of the American army—led by General Albert Sidney Johnson. It was to have been the Thermopylæ of Mormondom——but it wasn't. General Wells was to have done Leonidas——but he didn't.

A more cheerful view of the Desert.

The wild snow storms have left us—and we have thrown our wolf-skin overcoats aside. Certain tribes of far-western Indians bury their distinguished dead by placing them high in air and covering them with valuable furs——that is a very fair representation of these mid-air tombs. Those

On the right of the picture is the scaffold erected for an Indian grave. The corpse is placed on the top of it, out of the way of the wolves, though not so protected but what the vultures and other birds of carrion soon render it a mere skeleton.

animals are horses——I know they are—because my artist says so. I had the picture two years before I discovered the fact.——The artist came to me about six months ago—and said——" It is useless to disguise it from you any longer——they are horses."[a]

It was while crossing this desert that I was surrounded by a band of Ute Indians. They were splendidly mounted——they were dressed in beaver-skins——and they were armed with rifles—knives—and pistols.

What could I do?——What could a poor old orphan do? I'm a brave man.——The day before the Battle of Bull's Run I stood in the highway while the bullets——those dreadful messengers of death—— were passing all around me thickly——IN WAGGONS——on

---

[a] *They are Horses.*" Here again Artemus called in the aid of pleasant banter as the most fitting apology for the atrocious badness of the painting.

their way to the battle field.³² But there were too many of these Injuns————there were forty of them—and only one of me——and so I said—

"Great Chief—I surrender." His name was Wocky-bocky.

He dismounted—and approached me. I saw his tomahawk glisten in the morning sunlight.

Fire was in his eye. Wocky-bocky came very close to me and seized me by the hair of my head. He mingled his swarthy fingers with my golden

---

³² "*Their way to the battle-field.*" This was the great joke of Artemus Ward's first lecture, "The Babes in the Wood." He never omitted it in any of his lectures, nor did it lose its power to create laughter by repetition. The audiences at the Egyptian Hall, London, laughed as immoderately at it as did those of Irving Hall, New York, or of the Tremont Temple in Boston.

Utah Territory contains Indians of two races—the Shoshones and the Utes. The Utes are very friendly with the Mormons, who treat them with uniform kindness. It is commonly believed that a secret treaty of alliance exists between Brigham Young and the chiefs of the Indian tribes. (The left hand portion of the illustration belongs to the preceding picture.)

tresses——and he rubbed his dreadful Thomashawk across my lily-white face. He said—

"Torsha arrah darrah mishky bookshean!"

I told him he was right.

Wocky-bocky again rubbed his tomahawk across my face, and said—"Wink-ho—loo-boo!"

Says I—"Mr. Wocky-bocky"—says I——"Wocky—I have thought so for years—and so's all our family."

He told me I must go the tent of the Strong-Heart—and eat raw dog.[33] It don't agree with me. I prefer simple food. I prefer pork-pie—because then I know what I'm eating.

---

[33] "*Raw dog.*" While sojourning for a day in a camp of Sioux Indians we were informed that the warriors of the tribe were accustomed to eat raw dog to give them courage previous to going to battle. Artemus was greatly amused with the information. When, in after years, he became weak and languid, and was called upon to go to lecture, it was a favourite joke with him to inquire, "Hingston, have you got any raw dog?"

But as raw dog was all they proposed to give to me—I had to eat it or starve. So at the expiration of two days I seized a tin plate and went to the chief's daughter—and I said to her in a silvery voice———in a kind of German-silvery voice———I said—

"Sweet child of the forest, the pale-face wants his dog."

There was nothing but his paws! I had paused too long! Which reminds me that time passes. A way which time has.

I was told in my youth to seize opportunity. I once tried to seize one. He was rich. He had diamonds on. As I seized him—he knocked me down. Since then I have learned that he who seizes opportunity sees the penitentiary.

The Rocky Mountains.

The view may recall to those who have seen it Mr. Bierstadt's celebrated picture. Unfortunately for us, when we crossed, every inch of the ground was covered with snow.

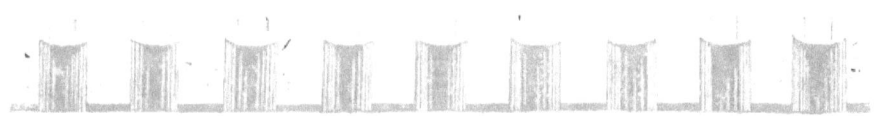

This picture is a continuation of the preceding view. In the course of the journey, Artemus Ward passed a day among an encampment of Sioux, whose numbers must have exceeded three thousand.

I take it for granted you have heard of these popular mountains. In America they are regarded as a great success, and we all love dearly to talk about them. It is a kind of weakness with us. I never knew but one American who hadn't something—sometime—to say about the Rocky Mountains——and he was a deaf and dumb man, who couldn't say anything about nothing.

But these mountains—whose summits are snow-covered and icy all the year round—are too grand to make fun of. I crossed them in the winter of '64—in a rough sleigh drawn by four mules.

This sparkling waterfall is the Laughing-Water alluded to by Mr. Longfellow in his Indian poem — "Higher - Water." The water is higher up there.

The plains of Colorado.

These are the dreary plains over which we rode for so many weary days. An affecting incident occurred on these plains some time since, which I am sure you will pardon me for introducing here.

On a beautiful June morning—some sixteen years ago—— —

(Music, very loud till the scene is off.)

⁂ ⁂ ⁂ ⁂ ⁂
⁂ ⁂ ⁂ ⁂
⁂ ⁂ ⁂ ⁂ ⁂
⁂ ⁂ ⁂ ⁂ ⁂

This view and the one which follows it convey a faint idea of the barrenness and desolation of a portion of the journey.

Nearly all the inhabitants of Salt Lake City have had to travel thither in emigrant trains, undergoing countless hardships on the way. The skeletons of animals and the remains of broken-down vehicles serve to mark out the track.

* * * * *
* * * * *
* * * * *
* * * * *
* * * * *
* * * * *
* * * * *
* * * * *
* * * * *
* * * * *
* * * * *
* * * * *

— — — —and she fainted on Reginald's breast![31]

[31] "*On Reginald's breast.*" At this part of the lecture Artemus pretended to tell a story—the piano playing loudly all the time. He continued his narration in excited dumb-show—his lips moving as though he were speaking. For some minutes the audience indulged in unrestrained laughter.

The Prairie on Fire.

A prairie on fire is one of the wildest and grandest sights that can possibly be imagined.

These fires occur—of course—in the summer—when the grass is dry as tinder——and the flames rush and roar over the prairie in a manner frightful to behold. They usually burn better than mine is burning to-night. I try to make my prairie burn regularly—and not disappoint the public——but it is not as high-principled as I am."[35]

---

[35] "*As high-principled as I am.*" The scene was a transparent one—the light from behind so managed as to give the

Artemus Ward had an opportunity of seeing part of a Prairie on Fire, just as he entered the State of Kansas. The grandeur of the scene made a very deep impression upon him. He frequently alluded to it in conversation.

THE PRAIRIE ON FIRE.

CONTINUED.

The effect of the Prairie being on Fire was illustrated in the panorama by means of a revolving cloth behind; a portion of the picture being transparent.

This is, of course, a mere fancy sketch. It was roughly designed by Artemus Ward himself. According to his own statement, made in a very playful manner, it represents that which he saw on an afternoon passed with the prophet at the palace.

Brigham Young at home.

The last picture I have to show you represents Mr. Brigham Young in the bosom of his family. His family is large — and the olive branches around his table are in a very tangled condition. He is more a father than any man I know. When at home——as you here see him——he ought to be very happy with sixty wives

effect of the prairie on fire. Artemus enjoyed the joke of letting the fire go out occasionally, and then allowing it to relight itself.

to minister to his comforts—and twice sixty children to soothe his distracted mind. Ah! my friends——what is home without a family?

What will become of Mormonism? We all know and admit it to be a hideous wrong———a great immoral stain upon the 'scutcheon of the United States. My belief is that its existence is dependent upon the life of Brigham Young. His administrative ability holds the system together ——his power of will maintains it as the faith of a community. When he dies—Mormonism will die too. The men who are around him have neither his talent nor his energy. By means of his strength it is held together. When he falls—Mormonism will also fall to pieces.

[36] That lion—you perceive—has a tail. It is a long one already. Like mine—it is to be continued in our next.[37]

THE END.

[36] "*That Lion has a tail.*" The lion on a pedestal, as painted in the panorama—its tail outstretched like that of the leonine adornment to Northumberland House, was a pure piece of frolic on the part of the entertainer. Brigham Young certainly adopts the lion as a Mormon emblem. A beehive and a lion, suggestive of industry and strength, are the symbols of the Mormons in Salt Lake City.

[37] "*To be continued in our next.*" To re-visit Utah, and to do another and a better lecture about it was a favourite idea of Artemus Ward. Another fancy that he had was to visit the

stranger countries of the Eastern world and find in some of them matter for a humorous lecture. While ill in Utah, he read Mr. Layard's book on Nineveh, left behind at the hotel by a traveller passing through Salt Lake. Mr. Layard's reference to the Yezedi, or "Devil worshippers," took powerful hold on the imagination of the reader. During our trip home across the plains he would often, sometimes in jest and sometimes in earnest, chat about a trip to Asia to see the "Devil worshippers." Naturally his inclinations were nomadic, and had a longer life been granted to him I believe that he would have seen more of the surface of this globe than even the generality of his countrymen see, much as they are accustomed to travel. Within about the same distance from Portland in England that his own birth-place is from Portland in Maine, his travels came to an end. He died at Southampton. His great wish was for strength to return to his home, that he might die with the face of his own mother bending over him, and in the cottage where he was born.

"Cœlumque
Adspicit et moriens dulces reminiscitur Argos."

E. P. H.

THE PROSCENIUM

WITH THE CURTAIN DOWN.

The curtain fell for the last time on Wednesday, the 23rd of January, 1867. Artemus Ward had to break off the lecture abruptly. He never lectured again.

APPENDIX.

"*THE TIMES*" NOTICE.

"EGYPTIAN HALL.—Before a large audience, comprising an extraordinary number of literary celebrities, Mr. Artemus Ward, the noted American humorist, made his first appearance as a public lecturer on Tuesday evening, the place selected for the display of his quaint oratory being the room long tenanted by Mr. Arthur Sketchley. His first entrance on the platform was the signal for loud and continuous laughter and applause, denoting a degree of expectation which a nervous man might have feared to encounter. However, his first sentences, and the way in which they were received, amply sufficed to prove that his success was certain. The dialect of Artemus bears a less evident mark of the Western World than that of many American actors, who would fain merge their own peculiarities in the delineation of English character; but his jokes are of that true Transatlantic type, to which no nation beyond the limits of the States can offer any parallel. These jokes he lets fall with an air of profound unconsciousness—we may almost say melancholy—which is irresistibly droll, aided as it is by the effect of a figure singularly gaunt and lean and a face to match. And he has found an audience by whom his caustic humour is thoroughly appreciated. Not one of the odd pleasantries slipped out with such imperturbable gravity misses its mark, and scarcely a minute elapses at the end of which the sedate Artemus is not forced to pause till the roar of mirth has subsided. There is certainly this foundation for an *entente cordiale* between the two countries calling themselves Anglo-Saxon, that the Englishman, puzzled by Yankee politics, thoroughly relishes Yankee jokes, though they are not in the least like his own. When two persons laugh together, they cannot hate each other much so long as the laugh continues.

The subject of Artemus Ward's lecture is a visit to the Mormons, copiously illustrated by a series of moving pictures, not much to be commended as works of art, but for the most part well enough executed to give (fidelity granted) a notion of life as it is among the remarkable inhabitants of Utah. Nor let the connoisseur, who detects the shortcomings of some of these pictures, fancy that he has discovered a flaw in the armour of the doughty Artemus. That astute gentleman knows their worth as well as anybody else, and while he ostensibly extols them, as a showman is bound to do, he every now and then holds them up to ridicule in a vein of the deepest irony. In one case a palpable error of perspective, by which a man is made equal in size to a mountain, has been purposely committed, and the shouts of laughter that arise as soon as the ridiculous picture appears is tremendous. But there is no mirth in the face of Artemus; he seems even deaf to the roar; and when he proceeds to the explanation of the landscape, he touches on the ridiculous point in a slurring way that provokes a new explosion.

The particulars of the lecture we need not describe. Many accounts of the Mormons, more or less credible, and all authenticated, have been given by serious historians, and Mr. W. H. Dixon, who has just returned from Utah to London, is said to have brought with him new stores of solid information. But to most of us Mormonism is still a mystery, and under those circumstances a lecturer who has professedly visited a country for the sake more of picking up fun than of sifting facts, and whose chief object it must be to make his narrative amusing, can scarcely be accepted as an authority. We will, therefore, content ourselves with stating that the lecture is entertaining to such a degree that to those who seek amusement its brevity is its only fault; that it is utterly free from offence, though the opportunities for offence given by the subject of Mormonism are obviously numerous; and that it is interspersed, not only with irresistible jokes, but with shrewd remarks, proving that Artemus Ward is a man of reflection, as well as a consummate humorist."

Every Night (except Saturday) at 8,

SATURDAY MORNINGS AT 3.

AMONG THE MORMONS.

During the Vacation the Hall has been carefully Swept out, and a new Door-Knob has been added to the Door.

Mr. Artemus Ward *will call on the Citizens of London, at their residences, and explain any jokes in his narrative which they may not understand.*

A person of long-established integrity will take excellent care of Bonnets, Cloaks, etc., during the Entertainment; the Audience better leave their money, however, with Mr. Ward; he will return it to them in a day or two, or invest it for them in America as they may think best.

☞ Nobody must say that he likes the Lecture unless he wishes to be thought eccentric ; and nobody must say that he doesn't like it unless he really *is* eccentric. (This requires thinking over, but it will amply repay perusal.)

The Panorama used to Illustrate Mr. WARD'S Narrative is rather worse than Panoramas usually are.

Mr. WARD will not be responsible for any debts of his own contracting.

PROGRAMME.

I.

APPEARANCE OF ARTEMUS WARD.

Who will be greeted with applause. ☞ The Stall-keeper is particularly requested to attend to this. ☞ When quiet has been restored, the Lecturer will present a rather frisky prologue, of about ten minutes in length, and of nearly the same width. It perhaps isn't necessary to speak of the depth.

II.

THE PICTURES COMMENCE HERE, the first one being a view of the California Steamship. Large crowd of citizens on the wharf, who appear to be entirely willing that ARTEMUS WARD shall go. "Bless you, Sir!" they say. "Don't hurry about coming back. Stay away for years, if you want to!" It was very touching. Disgraceful treatment of the passengers, who are obliged to go forward to smoke pipes, while the steamer herself is allowed 2 Smoke Pipes amid-ships. At Panama. A glance at Mexico.

III.
The Land of Gold.

Montgomery Street, San Francisco. The Gold Bricks. Street Scenes. "The Orphan Cabman, or The Mule Driver's Step-Father." The Chinese Theatre. Sixteen square-yards of a Chinese Comic Song.

IV.
The Land of Silver.

Virginia City, the wild young metropolis of the new Silver State. Fortunes are made there in a day. There are instances on record of young men going to this place without a shilling—poor and friendless—yet by energy, intelligence, and a careful disregard to business, they have been enabled to leave there, owing hundreds of pounds.

V.
The Great Desert at Night.

A dreary waste of sand. The sand isn't worth saving, however. Indians occupy yonder mountains. Little Injuns seen in the distance trundling their war-whoops.

VI.
A Bird's-eye View of Great Salt Lake City.

With some entirely descriptive talk.

VII.
Main Street, East Side.

The Salt Lake Hotel, which is conducted on Temperance principles. The landlord sells nothing stronger than salt butter.

VIII.
The Mormon Theatre.

The Lady of Lyons was produced here a short time since, but failed to satisfy a Mormon audience, on account of there being only one Pauline in it. The play was revised at once. It was presented the next night, with fifteen Paulines in the cast, and was a perfect success. ☞ All these statements may be regarded as strictly true. Mr. WARD would not deceive an infant.

IX.
Main Street, West Side.

This being a view of Main Street, West Side, it is naturally a view of the West Side of Main Street.

X.
Brigham Young's Harem.

Mr. Young is an indulgent father, and a numerous husband. For further particulars call on Mr. WARD, at Egyptian Hall, any Evening this Week. This paragraph is intended to blend business with amusement.

XI.
Heber C. Kimball's Harem.

We have only to repeat here the pleasant remarks above in regard to Brigham.

INTERMISSION OF FIVE MINUTES.

XII.
The Tabernacle.

XIII.
The Temple as it is.

XIV.
The Temple as it is to be.

XV.
The Great Salt Lake.

The Endowment House.

The Mormon is initiated into the mysteries of his faith here. The Mormon's religion is singular, and his wives are plural.

XVII.
Echo Canyon.

XVIII.
The Desert, again.

A more cheerful view. The Plains of Colorado. The Colorado Mountains "might have been seen" in the distance, if the Artist had painted 'em. But he is prejudiced against mountains, because his uncle once got lost on one.

XIX.

Brigham Young and his wives. The pretty girls of Utah mostly marry Young.

XX.
The Rocky Mountains.

XXI.
The Plains of Nebraska.

XXII.
The Prairie on Fire.

RECOMMENDATIONS.

TOTNES, Oct. 20th, 1866.

Mr. ARTEMUS WARD,

My dear Sir,—My wife was dangerously unwell for over sixteen years. She was so weak that she could not lift a teaspoon to her mouth. But in a fortunate moment she commenced reading one of your lectures. She got better at once. She gained strength so rapidly that she lifted the cottage piano quite a distance from the floor, and then tipped it over on to her mother-in-law, with whom she had had some little trouble. We like your lectures very much. Please send me a barrel of them. If you should require any more recommendations you can get any number of them in this place, at two shillings each, the price I charge for this one, and I trust you may be ever happy.

I am, Sir,

Yours truly, and so is my wife,

R. SPRINGERS.

An American correspondent of a distinguished journal in Yorkshire thus speaks of Mr. WARD's power as an Orator:—

"It was a grand scene, Mr ARTEMUS WARD standing on the platform, talking; many of the audience sleeping tranquilly in their seats; others leaving the room and not returning; others crying like a child at some of the jokes—all, all formed a most impressive scene, and showed the powers of this remarkable orator. And when he announced that he should never lecture in that town again, the applause was absolutely deafening."

Doors open at Half-past Seven, commence at Eight.
Conclude at Half-past Nine.

EVERY EVENING EXCEPT SATURDAY.

SATURDAY AFTERNOONS at 3 p.m.

His Programme.

Dodworth Hall, 806, Broadway.

OPEN EVERY EVENING.

1.—Introductory.
2.—The Steamer Ariel, en route.
3.—San Francisco.
4.—The Washoe Silver Region.
5.—The Plains.
6.—The City of Saints.
7.—A Mormon Hotel.
8.—Brigham Young's Theatre.
9.—The Council-House.
10.—The Home of Brigham Young.
11.—Heber C. Kimball's Seraglio.
12.—The Mormon House of Worship.
13.—Foundations of the New Temple.
14.—Architect's View of the Temple when finished.
15.—The Great Dead Sea of the Desert.
16.—The House of Mystery.
17.—The Canon.
18.—Mid-Air Sepulture.
19.—A Nice Family Party at Brigham Young's.

It requires a large number of Artists to produce this Entertainment. The casual observer can form no idea of the quantity of unfettered genius that is soaring, like a healthy Eagle, round this Hall in connection with this Entertainment. In fact, the following gifted persons compose the

Official Bureau.

Secretary of the Exterior .... Mr. E. P. Hingston.
Secretary of the Treasury.............. ....Herr Max Field,
(Pupil of Signor Thomaso Jacksoni.)
Mechanical Director and Professor of Carpentry...... Signor G. Wilsoni.
Crankist............................. ....Mons. Aleck.
Assistant Crankist.................................. Boy (orphan).
Artists ....Messrs. Hilliard & Meader.
Reserved Chairists ....Messrs. Persee & Jerome.
Moppist ....Signorina O'Flaherty.
Broomist ....Mlle. Topsia de St. Moke.
Hired Man ....John.
Fighting Editor .... Chevalier McArone.
Dutchman .... By a Polish Refugee, named McFinnigin.
Doortendist .... Mons. Jacques Ridere.
Gas Man .... Artemus Ward.

This Entertainment will open with music. The Soldiers' Chorus from "Faust." First time in this city.

***

Next comes a jocund and discursive preamble, calculated to show what a good education the Lecturer has.

***

View the first is a sea-view.—Ariel navigation.—Normal school of whales in the distance.—Isthmus of Panama.—Interesting interview with Old Panama himself, who makes all the hats. Old Pan. is a likely sort of man.

***

San Francisco.—City with a vigilant government.—Miners allowed to vote. Old inhabitants so rich that they have legs with golden calves to them.

Town in the Silver region.—Good quarters to be found there.—Playful population, fond of high-low-jack and homicide.—Silver lying around loose.—Thefts of it termed silver-guilt.

.*.

The Plains in Winter.—A wild Moor, like Othello.—Mountains in the distance forty thousand miles above the level of the highest sea (Musiani's chest C included).—If you don't believe this you can go there and measure them for yourself.

.*.

Mormondom, sometimes called the City of the Plain, but wrongly; the women are quite pretty.—View of Old Poly Gamy's house, &c.

.*.

The Salt Lake Hotel.—Stage just come in from its overland route and retreat from the Indians.—Temperance house.—No bar nearer than Salt Lake sand-bars.—Miners in shirts like Artemus Ward his Programme—they are read and will wash.

.*.

. . . Theatre, where Artemus Ward lectured.—Mormons like . . . . and had rather go to the Play-house than to the Work-house, any time.—Private boxes reserved for the ears of Brother Brigham's wives.

.*.

Intermission of Five Minutes.

.*.

Territorial State-House.—Seat of the Legislature.—About as fair a collection as that at Albany—and we "can't say no fairer than that."

.*.

Residence of Brigham Young and his wives.—Two hundred souls with but a single thought, Two hundred hearts that beat as one.

Seraglio of Heber C. Kimball.—Home of the Queens of Heber.—No relatives of the Queen of Sheba.—They are a nice gang of darlings.

**

Mormon Tabernacle, where the men espouse Mormonism and the women espouse Brother Brigham and his Elders as spiritual Physicians, convicted of bad doct'rin.

**

Foundations of the Temple.—Beginning of a healthy little job.—Temple to enclose all out-doors, and be paved with gold at a premium.

**

The Temple when finished.—Mormon idea of a meeting-house.—N.B. It will be bigger, probably, than Dodworth Hall.—One of the figures in the foreground is intended for Heber C. Kimball.—You can see, by the expression of his back, that he is thinking what a great man Joseph Smith was.

**

The Great Salt Lake.—Water actually thick with salt—too saline to sail in.—Mariners rocked on the bosom of this deep with rock salt.—The water isn't very good to drink.

**

House where Mormons are initiated.—Very secret and mysterious ceremonies.—Anybody can easily find out all about them though, by going out there and becoming a Mormon.

**

Echo Cañon. — A rough bluff sort of affair.—Great Echo.—When Artemus Ward went through, he heard the echoes of some things the Indians said there about four years and a half ago.

**

The Plains again, with some noble savages, both in the live and dead state.—The dead one on the high shelf was killed in a Fratricidal Struggle.—They are always having Fratricidal Struggles out in that line of country.—It would be a good place for an enterprising Coroner to locate.

.*.

Brigham Young surrounded by his wives.—These ladies are simply too numerous to mention.

.*.

☞ Those of the Audience who do not feel offended with Artemus Ward are cordially invited to call upon him, often, at his fine new house in Brooklyn. His house is on the right hand side as you cross the Ferry, and may be easily distinguished from the other houses by its having a Cupola and a Mortgage on it.

.*.

☞ Soldiers on the battle-field will be admitted to this Entertainment gratis.

.*.

☞ The Indians on the Overland Route live on Routes and Herbs. They are an intemperate people. They drink with impunity, or anybody who invites them.

.*.

☞ Artemus Ward delivered Lectures before

ALL THE CROWNED HEADS OF EUROPE

ever thought of delivering lectures.

TICKETS 50 CTS. RESERVED CHAIRS $1.

Doors open at 7.30 P.M.; Entertainment to commence at 8.

☞ The Piano used is from the celebrated factory of Messrs. CHICKERING & SONS, 653, Broadway.

The Cabinet Organ is from the famous factory of Messrs. MASON & HAMLIN, Boston, and is furnished by MASON BROTHERS, 7 Mercer Street, New York.

JUDD AND GLASS, PRINTERS, PHŒNIX WORKS, LONDON.

THE
GENIAL SHOWMAN;

BEING REMINISCENCES OF

THE LIFE OF ARTEMUS WARD,

AND

PICTURES OF A SHOWMAN'S CAREER

IN THE WESTERN WORLD.

BY

EDWARD P. HINGSTON.

VERY IMPORTANT NEW BOOKS.

AARON PENLEY'S Sketching in Water Colours,

for 21s. By AARON PENLEY, Author of "The English School of Painting in Water-Colours," &c. ILLUSTRATED WITH TWENTY-ONE BEAUTIFUL CHROMO-LITHOGRAPHS, produced with the utmost care to resemble original WATER-COLOUR DRAWINGS. Small folio, the text tastefully printed, in handsome binding, gilt edges, suitable for the drawing-room table, price 21s.

*** It has long been felt that the magnificent work of the great English master of painting in water-colours, published at £4 4s., was too dear for general circulation. The above embodies all the instructions of the distinguished author, with twenty-one beautiful specimens of water-colour painting.

A Clever and Brilliant Book (*Companion to the "Bon Gaultier Ballads"*) PUCK ON PEGASUS. By H. CHOLMONDELEY PENNELL.

"*** This most amusing work has already passed through FIVE EDITIONS, receiving everywhere the highest praise as "a clever and brilliant book." TO NO OTHER WORK OF THE PRESENT DAY HAVE SO MANY DISTINGUISHED ARTISTS CONTRIBUTED ILLUSTRATIONS. To the designs of GEORGE CRUIKSHANK, JOHN LEECH, JULIAN PORTCH, "PHIZ," and other artists, SIR NOEL PATON, MILLAIS, JOHN TENNIEL, RICHARD DOYLE, and M. ELLEN EDWARDS have now contributed several exquisite pictures, thus making the new edition—which is TWICE THE SIZE OF THE OLD ONE, and contains irresistibly funny pieces—THE BEST BOOK FOR THE DRAWING-ROOM TABLE NOW PUBLISHED.

In 4to, printed within an india-paper tone, and elegantly bound, gilt, gilt edges, price 10s. 6d. only.

John Camden Hotten, 74 and 75, Piccadilly, W.

VERY IMPORTANT NEW BOOKS.

THE NEW "PUNIANA SERIES" OF
CHOICE ILLUSTRATED WORKS OF HUMOUR.

Elegantly printed on toned paper, full gilt, gilt edges, for the Drawing Room, price 6s. each:—

1. **Carols of Cockayne. By Henry S. Leigh.** Vers de Société, and charming Verses descriptive of London life. With numerous exquisite little designs by ALFRED CONCANEN and the late JOHN LEECH. Small 4to, elegant, uniform with "Puniana," 6s.

2. **The "Bab Ballads." New Illustrated Book of** HUMOUR; OR, A GREAT DEAL OF RHYME WITH VERY LITTLE REASON. By W. S. GILBERT. WITH A MOST LAUGHABLE ILLUSTRATION ON NEARLY EVERY PAGE, DRAWN BY THE AUTHOR. On toned paper, gilt edges, price 6s.

"An awfully Jolly Book for Parties."

3. **Puniana. Best Book of Riddles and Puns ever** formed. Thoughts Wise—and Otherwise. With nearly 100 exquisitely fanciful drawings. Contains nearly 3,000 of the best Riddles and 10,000 most outrageous Puns, and is one of the most popular books ever issued. New edition, uniform with the "Bab Ballads," price 6s.

Why did Du Chaillu get so angry when he was chaffed about the Gorilla? Why? we ask.
Why is a chrysalis like a hot roll? You will doubtless remark, "Because it's the grub that makes the butter fly!" But see "Puniana."
Why is a wide awake hat so called? Because it never had a nap, and never wants one.

The *Saturday Review* says of this most amusing work—"Enormous burlesque—unapproachable and pre-eminent. We venture to think that this very queer volume will be a favourite. It deserves to be ... and we should suggest that, to a dull person desirous to get credit with the young holiday people, it would be good policy to invest in the book, and dole it out by instalments."

John Camden Hotten, 74 and 75, Piccadilly, W.

VERY IMPORTANT NEW BOOKS.

Seymour's Sketches. A Companion Volume to
"Leech's Pictures." The Book of Cockney Sports, Whims, and Oddities. Nearly 200 highly amusing Illustrations. Oblong 4to, a handsome volume, half morocco, price 12s.

⁎ A re-issue of the famous pictorial comicalities which were so popular thirty years ago. The volume is admirably adapted for a table-book, and the pictures will doubtless again meet with that popularity which was extended towards them when the artist projected with Mr. Dickens the famous "Pickwick Papers."

The Famous "DOCTOR SYNTAX'S" Three Tours.
One of the most Amusing and Laughable Books ever published. With the whole of Rowlandson's very droll full-page illustrations, *in colours, after the original drawings.* Comprising the well-known Tours:—

1. In Search of the Picturesque.
2. In Search of Consolation.
3. In Search of a Wife.

The three series complete and unabridged from the original editions in one handsome volume, with a Life of this industrious Author—the English Le Sage—now first written by John Camden Hotten.

⁎ It is not a little surprising that the most voluminous and popular English writer since the days of Defoe should never before have received the small honour of a biography. *This Edition contains the whole of the original, hitherto sold for £1 11s. 6d., but which is now published at* **7s. 6d. only.**

A VERY USEFUL BOOK. In folio, half morocco, cloth sides, 7s. 6d.
Literary Scraps, Cuttings from Newspapers, Ex-
tracts, Miscellanea, &c. *A FOLIO SCRAP-BOOK OF 340 COLUMNS,* formed for the reception of Cuttings, &c., with guards.

☞ *Authors and literary men have thanked the publisher for this useful book.*

⁎ A most useful volume, and one of the cheapest ever sold. The book is sure to be appreciated, and to become popular.

Hone's Scrap Book. A Supplementary Volume to
the "Every-Day Book," the "Year-Book," and the "Table-Book." From the MSS. of the late WILLIAM HONE, with upwards of One Hundred and Fifty engravings of curious or eccentric objects. Thick 8vo, uniform with "Year-Book," pp. 800. [*In preparation.*

John Camden Hotten, 74 and 75, Piccadilly, W.

www.ingramcontent.com/pod-product-compliance
Lightning Source LLC
Chambersburg PA
CBHW021304240426

43669CB00042B/1108